Florida A&M University, Tallahassee
Florida Atlantic University, Boca Raton
Florida Gulf Coast University, Ft. Myers
Florida International University, Miami
Florida State University, Tallahassee
University of Central Florida, Orlando
University of Florida, Gainesville
University of North Florida, Jacksonville
University of South Florida, Tampa
University of West Florida, Pensacola

Journeys with Florida's Indians

UPF

Young Readers Library

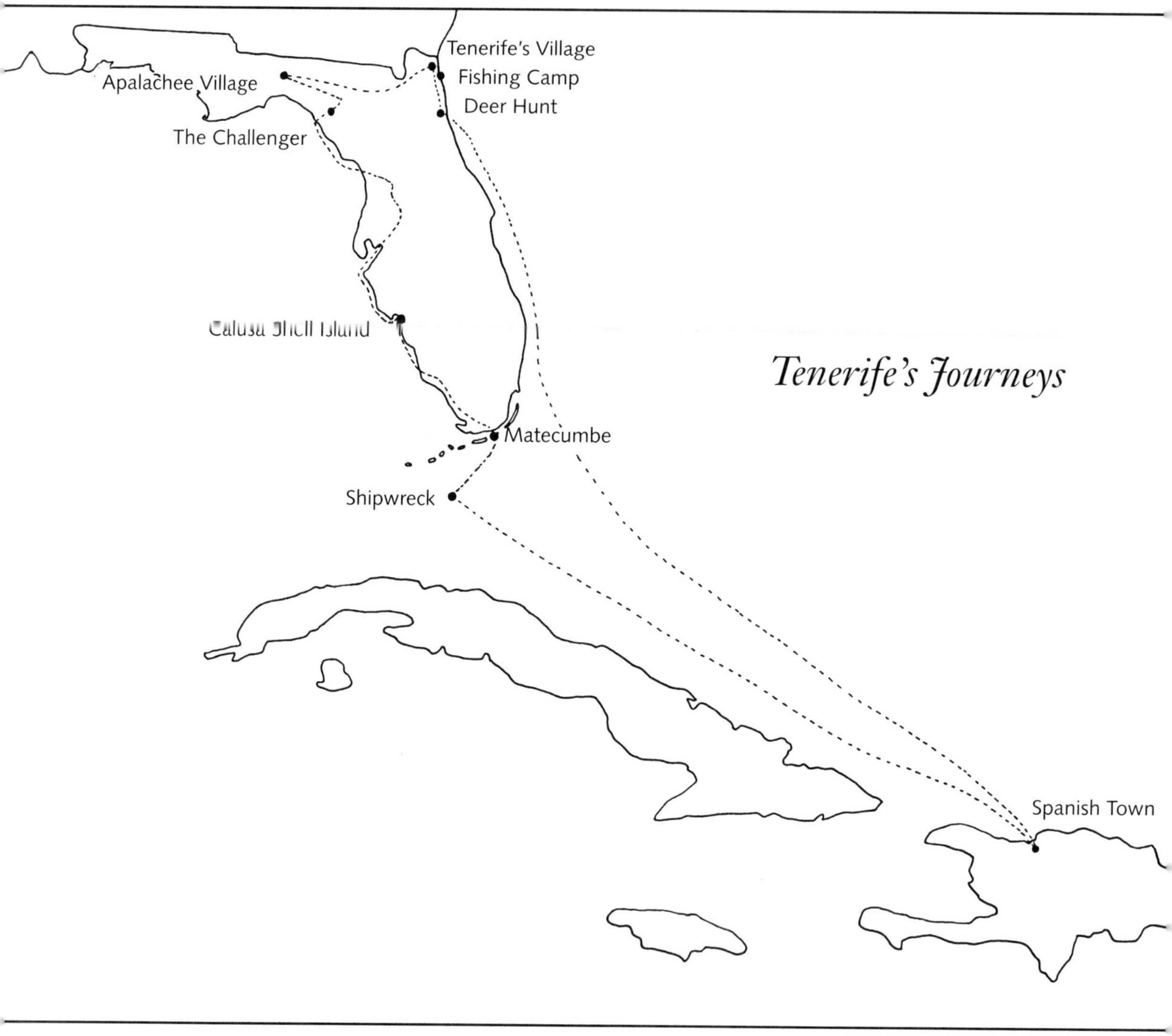

Tenerife's Village
Fishing Camp
Deer Hunt
Apalachee Village
The Challenger
Calusa Shell Island
Tenerife's Journeys
Matecumbe
Shipwreck
Spanish Town

Journeys with Florida's Indians

Kelley G. Weitzel

University Press of Florida

Gainesville · Tallahassee · Tampa · Boca Raton

Pensacola · Orlando · Miami · Jacksonville · Ft. Myers

07 06 05 04 03 02 6 5 4 3 2 1

Library of Congress Cataloging-in-Publication Data
Weitzel, Kelley G., 1969–
Journeys with Florida's Indians / Kelley G. Weitzel
p. cm.
Summary: Describes the history and culture of the native peoples of Florida, including the Timucua, Calusa, and Apalachee.
Includes bibliographical references and index.
ISBN 0-8130-2581-8 (c.: alk. paper)
1. Indians of North America—Florida—Juvenile literature. [1. Indians of North America—Florida.] I. Title.
E78.F6 W44 2002
975.9'00497—dc21 2002071465

The University Press of Florida is the scholarly publishing agency for the State University System of Florida, comprising Florida A&M University, Florida Atlantic University, Florida Gulf Coast University, Florida International University, Florida State University, University of Central Florida, University of Florida, University of North Florida, University of South Florida, and University of West Florida.

University Press of Florida
15 Northwest 15th Street
Gainesville, FL 32611–2079
http://www.upf.com

This book is dedicated to Sheko, Kidawe, Ashefa, and Hassalla,

who inspire me to reach for the past and the future.

Contents

Note: The chapter titles in *italic* indicate a fictional chapter.

Figures

Preface

Journeys with Florida's Indians has factual and fictional chapters. The factual chapters are full of pictures, maps, and information about Florida's Indians. The fictional chapters tell stories about the fire drives, shark hunts, and native ball games that made up the daily lives of Florida's first people. These stories are designed for upper-elementary and middle school readers, but they can be read aloud for younger children too. For any reader, *Journeys with Florida's Indians* is a book and an adventure all in one.

Many people shared their time and talents on this project. Jerald Milanich, William Marquardt, John Hann, and Bonnie McEwan provided excellent critiques. The Pelotes Island Nature Preserve staff provided support and artwork. These naturalists include Erin Clary, Lesley Royce, Heather Shuke, Rachelle Marker, Christina Zabinski, and Tammy Cooper.

I owe personal thanks to my writing mentor, Kathy Hassall, who speaks the truth with kindness, to Kimber Herrera, the best friend a sister can be, and to Sheldon Pantin, my partner in all things.

Chronology

When Did Important Things Happen?

15,000 years ago	Paleo-Indians cross the Bering Land Bridge into North America.
12,000 years ago	Paleo-Indians arrive in Florida.
9,500 years ago	Archaic Indians live in Florida.
2,500 years ago	Woodland Indians have settled in all parts of Florida, later becoming Apalachee, Calusa, Timucua, and other native cultures.
500+ years ago	Columbus lands in the West Indies and "discovers" the Americas.
400+ years ago	The French and Spanish build forts and missions in Florida.
230+ years ago	Most of Florida's Indians have disappeared as a result of disease or slave raids. Some of those who survive leave Florida.
Today	Young readers get a chance to see what life was like for Florida Indians long ago.

Introduction

How Is This Book Set Up?

In this book, you will see the words "Indian," "native people," and "Native American." These names describe people who lived in North and South America BEFORE and AFTER the Europeans arrived. This book focuses on the native groups that lived in Florida. Did Florida's early people have dogs as pets? How big were their houses? What kinds of spear points did they make?

We've found the answers to these questions with the help of **archaeologists** and **historians**. Archaeologists learn by studying **artifacts**, including pottery, spear points, and food trash. Historians discover facts about these Indians by reading descriptive letters and stories. These documents were written by Europeans visiting the **New World** long ago. (Have you noticed the words in **bold text**? These words and their definitions can be found in the glossary, starting on page 213.)

In this book, you will read some factual chapters and some fictional stories. For example, you will read a factual chapter called "**Paleo-Indians**," then a story about a Paleo-Indian mammoth hunt. To find out which chapters are stories, look at the "Contents" on page ix. The titles of story chapters are in *italics*; factual chapters are in plain text.

You'll meet many characters in the following story chapters. Some of these characters are fictional, but others actually lived in Florida in the 1500s. Atore, Calos, Saturiwa, Senquene, and Ribault were as real as you are. The other story characters are not real people. However, the places they live, the clothing they wear, and the things they do are based on real historical and archaeological facts. Reading stories like these can help you imagine the lifestyles of Florida's early native people.

The fictional chapters in this book have a main character named Tenerife (Ten-eh-REE-feh). He tells stories like "Springing the Trap" and "Shark Hunt" to people in his village. *When you see words in italics, like this,* you know Tenerife is telling a story.

Exploring this book will lead you on adventures across Florida. With Tenerife, you'll be captured by the Spanish and live as a slave of the fierce Calusa people. You'll hunt sharks and make a daring escape as you struggle to find your way home. The factual chapters will get you ready for each adventure. As you begin to read, you will step back almost five hundred years in time—to the year A.D. 1527. You will learn to survive in wild Florida and find out if you would have liked being a Timucua, Calusa, or Apalachee Indian. Turn the page and join the adventure.

The Chase

New characters in this section:

Tenerife (Ten-eh-REE-feh): An eight-year-old Timucua boy

Ashefa (Uh-SHE-fuh): A nine-year-old Timucua girl

Saturiwa (Sa-chur-EE-wa): A twelve-year-old Timucua boy, the chief's nephew

Jote (JOE-teh): An excellent toolmaker

Tenerife ran faster than he had in all of his eight **winters**. He swerved past the guard hut and cut right through the middle of the village. He only had to make it to his grandmother's hut. The boy craned his neck around, looking for Ashefa. Where was she? She had been right behind him. Tenerife felt his leg muscles starting to tire and struggled to run even faster. He glanced back again. Where was she?

He could not waste time wondering.

Tenerife leaped over a pile of firewood, gripping the stone point he'd just found. He glanced back again, but Ashefa was nowhere in sight. Where could she be? Tenerife dodged around his mother's hut and kept on running. What if Ashefa had taken a short cut? Tenerife

---

Note: The name "Tenerife" means "mountains" in Granberry's Timucua dictionary. It is also the name of a Spanish island off the northwest coast of Africa. Historians are not sure if there is a connection between these two names.

knew one too. He swerved left, cutting behind the **council house**—and slammed straight into Saturiwa.

The chief's nephew grabbed Tenerife's shoulders and pushed him to the ground. "Who are you running from, shrimp? Your little girlfriend?"

Tenerife tightened his grip on the stone point, but said nothing. Fighting back wouldn't help. Saturiwa was big, and he was the chief's nephew.

The bully grinned and held Tenerife's face and shoulders to the ground. "He's over here, Ashefa!" Saturiwa shouted.

Tenerife tasted dirt on his lips and struggled to pull free. If he didn't get away soon, Ashefa would catch him for sure. Finally, he scrambled away from Saturiwa. When he got to the far side of the council house, Ashefa was sprinting toward him! Tenerife took three leaping steps through his grandmother's garden and slid right through the doorway of her hut.

Ashefa dashed in behind him, swishing the edges of the palm-**frond** walls. "Your grandmother's not here to protect you," she said. "Give it here!" Ashefa grabbed for the stone spear point, but Tenerife yanked it away.

He waved the stone point in front of her face. "Beat you!"

"You wouldn't have found that point except for me," she said. "It was my idea to hunt oysters in the south marsh. Besides, I should get it. I'm older."

"So what!" Tenerife said. "Only by a winter. And you're a girl."

Ashefa's voice was low. "Tenerife, give me the point."

Tenerife folded his arms across his chest the way the bigger boys did. He shook his head.

"I'll bet you," she said.

"What kind of bet?"

"About why the point is made of dark gray stone instead of white **chert** stone. Right answer keeps it. Deal?"

Tenerife thought about it and nodded. "Deal. It's because the point sat in the marsh mud for so long. That's why it's so dark."

"Ha!" she shouted. "Give me the point. It's like I said before. The stone comes from far away. I just asked Jote."

"You didn't have time to ask him!" Tenerife said.

"Did too! How else do you think you beat me here?" Ashefa jumped up and danced around him. "I told you. I'm smarter than you are. I'm smarter than you are."

"Cut it out!" Tenerife shouted.

But Ashefa did not cut it out. She was just getting started. "I can't believe you thought it was the mud!" she laughed. The girl twirled around twice and dipped her hand in the water pot. She flicked droplets in Tenerife's face and twirled again.

Tenerife spun around and glared at her. "You think you're smarter?" he said. "Well, I'm stronger."

And he gave her a shove. Not a hard shove, but Ashefa was so busy dancing around, she was already off balance. She started falling toward the cooking fire.

"Ashefa!" Tenerife called. He threw the stone point aside and tried to catch her, but . . .

What happens to Tenerife and Ashefa? You'll find out when the adventure continues.

Florida's First People

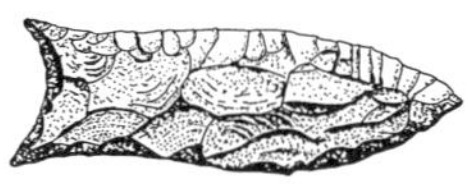

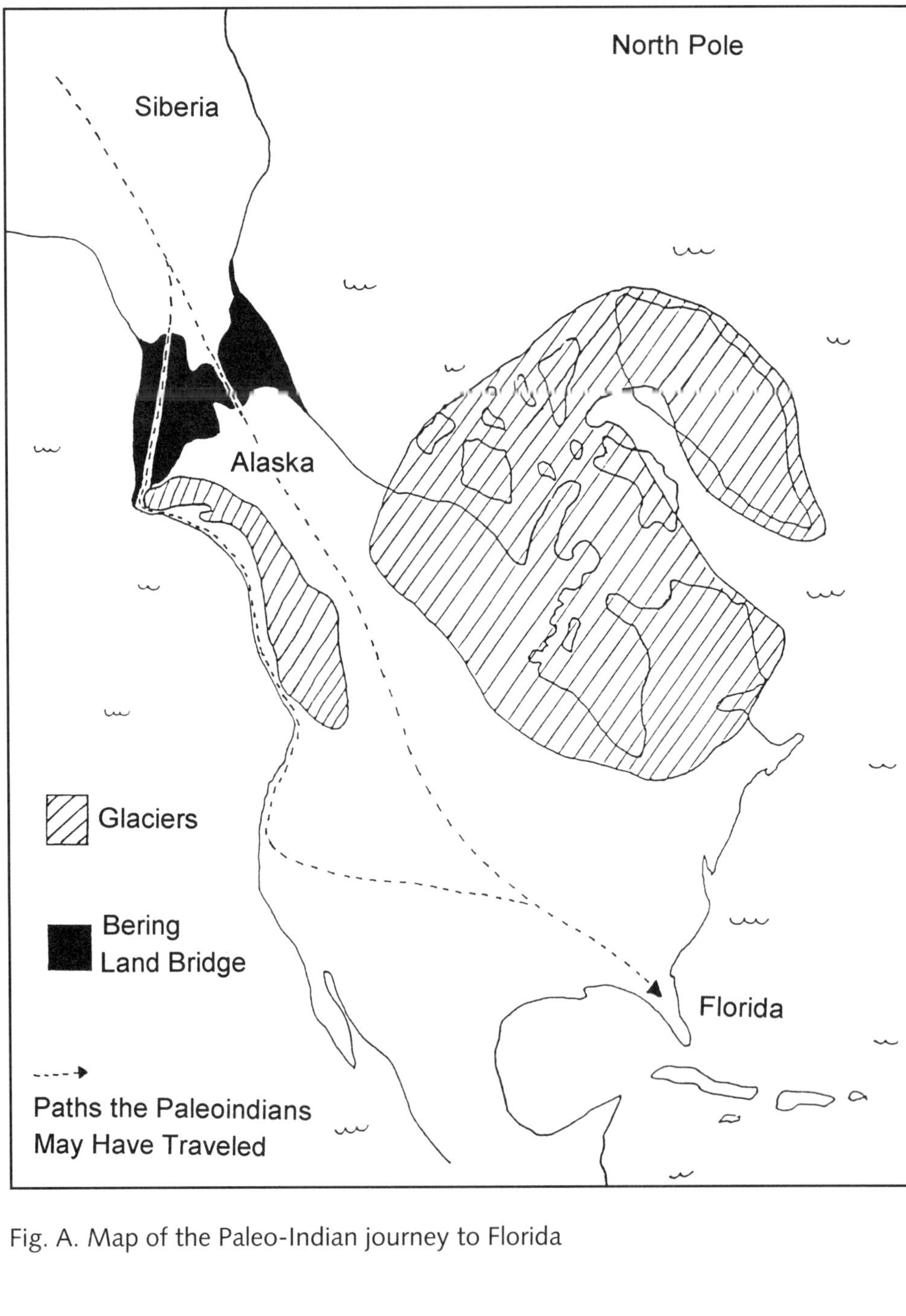

Fig. A. Map of the Paleo-Indian journey to Florida

1

Paleo-Indians

Florida's first native people were called **Paleo-Indians**. At least 12,000 years ago, they made their way into the land we call Florida. These people had walked a long way. Their great-great-great-grandmothers and grandfathers had started the journey long ago in Siberia. (See figure A.)

The Paleo-Indians were **nomads** and traveled around for three main reasons. First, they moved to find better weather. They looked for warmer places in the winter and cooler places in the summer.

Second, they moved to find plant foods and dry firewood. If they stayed in the same place too long, they used up all of the wild fruits and dead wood. There would be nothing left to eat or burn as fuel. The Paleo-Indians did not know how to plant gardens, so they had to eat whatever grew naturally. When the wild plant foods ran out, they had to find a new place to live.

Third, the Paleo-Indians traveled to follow the herds of large animals they hunted, including mammoths, bison, and horses. These **megafauna** were also searching for better weather and plant foods. The searching animals traveled right up through Siberia onto a strip of land called the Bering Land Bridge. (Look back at figure A.) Siberia is on the northeast side of Asia. Alaska is on the northwest side of North America. The Bering Land Bridge hooks them together.

Today, most of the space between Siberia and Alaska is under water. But 15,000 years ago, much of the earth's water was frozen into **glaciers**, which made the ocean's water levels drop very low. In some places, like the area between Siberia and Alaska, the ocean floor was completely dry. The Paleo-Indians walked right over the dry ocean bottom on a path a thousand miles wide. They followed the **migrating** megafauna right into North America.

Over thousands of years, the Paleo-Indians traveled to many parts of North and South America. Some learned to hunt buffalo and build teepees, like the Sioux who settled in the Great Plains. Other Paleo-Indians went into Central and South America. Their descendents built giant stone cities, as the Incas did in Peru. The Paleo-Indians who settled in Florida eventually developed into many different native cultures, like the Apalachee, the Calusa, and the Timucua.

What is a culture? Your culture is your way of life. It means the ways you find food, the kinds of jobs men and women have, the ways you cook, the types of houses you build, your religion, your clothes, your language, and everything else that makes your people special. Everyone has a culture. The culture in a small town is different from the culture in a big city.

What was the Paleo-Indian culture like? These ancient people lived in tribes of about 25 people. They probably had a male leader. In addition to leading, he also hunted animals for food and protected the tribe. With only 25 people in the tribe, each person had to do his or her part.

The men hunted megafauna such as bison and mammoths, but also smaller animals, including raccoons, foxes, deer, turtles, birds, and fish. Paleo-Indian women probably hunted small animals too. In fact, the women provided up to 65 percent of their people's food by collecting berries, leaves, grains, nuts, small animals, and eggs.

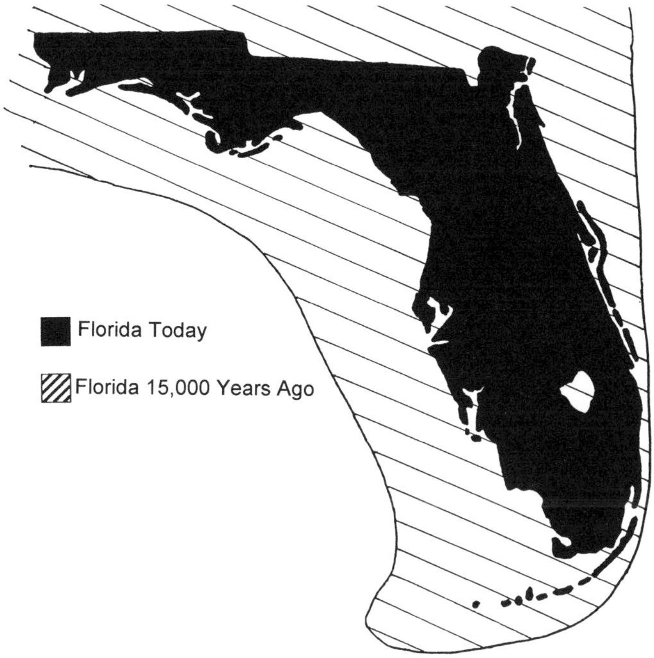

Fig. B. Map of Florida in Paleo-Indian times

Since every man and woman was needed to find enough food, no person was more important than anyone else. The best hunter led the hunt. The best toolmaker trained others to make better tools. The only way they could survive was if everyone cooperated.

When the Paleo-Indians arrived in Florida, oceans covered less of the land. In fact, 10,000 years ago, Florida was about twice as big as it is today. (See figure B.) Most of Florida was a grassy prairie, with very few rivers, lakes, or trees. This dry landscape provided good living space for megafauna like mammoths and bison.

The only sources of fresh water were a few rivers and **sinkholes**. Plenty of trees, shrubs, and grasses grew near these water sources. The water and plants attracted large animals, like mammoths, as well as small animals, like raccoons and rabbits. Many Paleo-Indians made their homes near these sources of water and food. Near sinkholes, they also found **chert,** a whitish-gray stone used to make spear points.

The kind of chert point usually made in Paleo-Florida was a Suwannee point. (See figure C.) This point could be made into a knife or spearhead. Look at the C shaped curve at the end of the Suwannee point. Paleo-points usually have that curve.

In addition to chert, Paleo-Indians used other tool-making materials, including wood, bone, and tusk. Knives, **mortars** for grinding seeds, and hunting boomerangs (bent clubs that did *not* return to the thrower) were all made from wood. The Paleo-Indians also carved spear points and fishhooks from pieces of bone and mammoth tusk. They were constantly moving into new environments and inventing technologies (like better hunting points) to help them face each challenge they met. Keep reading to find out how these new technologies changed Florida's first people.

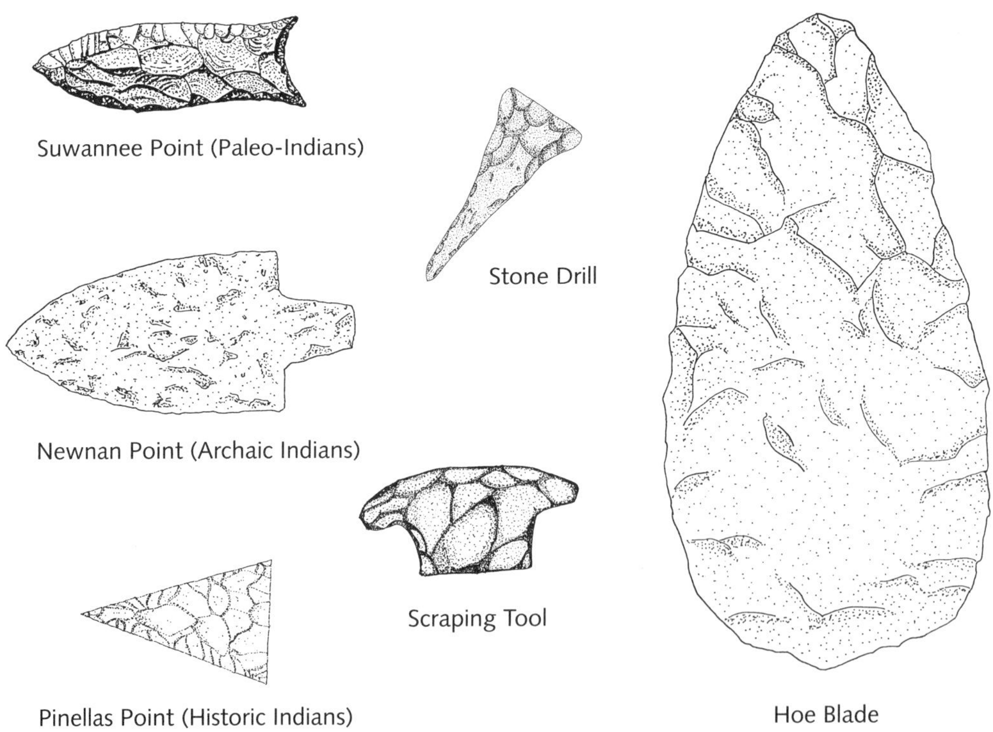

Fig. C. Florida projectile points

2

Archaic Indians

About 8,000 years ago, the earth started warming up. This extra heat melted some of the glaciers and raised the levels of the ocean. Higher ocean levels made Florida a much smaller place. By 5,000 years ago, Florida was only half as big as it had been. (Look back at figure B on page 11.)

As ocean levels rose, many Paleo-Indian home sites were covered by seawater. The people moved inland and made their homes near new rivers formed by the faraway melting glaciers. These people invented new ways to live and find food. Because their way of life was changing, archaeologists have given them a new name: Archaic Indians.

What made the Archaic Indians different? For one thing, they were not traveling around so much. They probably had a central village with special sites nearby for hunting deer, collecting oysters, and making tools.

The Archaic people hunted animals on water and on land. From the water, they got fish, alligators, and turtles, as well as **shellfish** such as oysters, whelks, and snails. On land, they hunted deer, raccoon, fox, turkey, and many other animals. (The megafauna had disappeared by this time.) Archaic people also ate many plant foods, including blueberries, grapes, hickory nuts, prickly pears, and pigweed seeds. With so much food close to their new homes, they did not have to travel anymore.

This gave Archaic Indians more time to invent new tools and come up with new ideas—like pottery. Shaping **slabs** of clay into bowls and hardening them in a fire was a huge discovery for the Archaic Indians. Pottery was a much more effective tool for cooking soups and stews than the animal skin pots used by the Paleo-Indians. Pottery also improved food storage, because it kept mice, bugs, and moisture away from the food. (See figure D.)

Archaic Indians also discovered a new material they could use

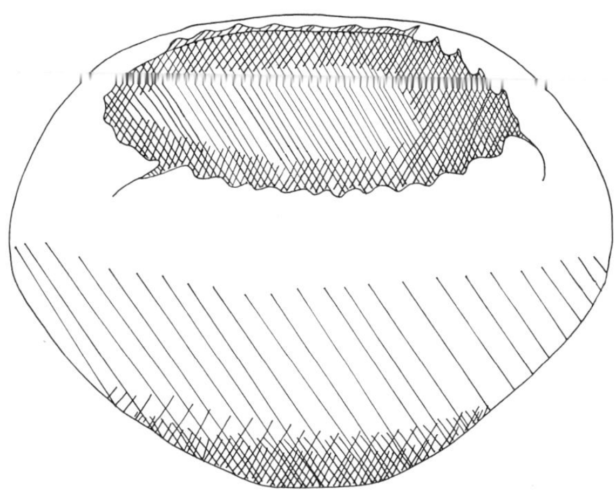

Native Pot

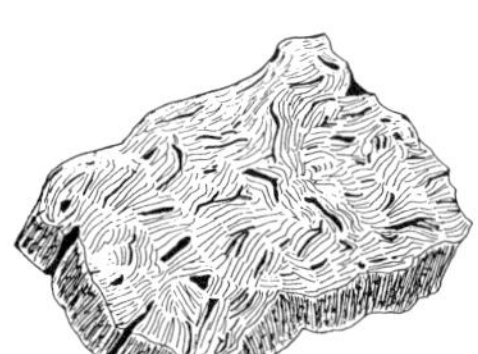

A Piece of Fiber-tempered Pottery

A Piece of Sand-tempered Pottery with a Check-stamp Design

Fig. D. Florida pottery. Archaic Indians made heavy "**fiber-tempered**" pottery by shaping a layer or slab of clay. Historic Indians made lighter pottery by coiling the clay. When they added sand to the clay they **coiled**, it was called "sand-tempered" pottery.

for making tools—shell. They ate the animal inside each shell, then made the shells into grinders, choppers, axes, shell cups, ear decorations, and weights for fishing nets. The rest of the shells were thrown in trash piles that grew to twenty feet high. (Look ahead to figures M and R on pages 44 and 55 to see examples of shell tools and **middens**.)

The spear thrower, or **atlatl** (at-LAT-el), was another Archaic tool. It allowed hunters to throw a spear much farther than they could using just the strength of their arm. Archaic Indians also learned to use traps, **snares**, **weirs**, and nets. Each of these tools helped them capture animals without having to chase them down. Archaic people could spend less time hunting and more time on other activities, like toolmaking.

They learned that heating chert stone made it easier to chip and shape. Many tools were made with this new, easier method, including atlatl points, knives, drills, hoes, and scrapers. (You can see some of these in figure C on page 12.)

Another Archaic invention was the **dugout** canoe. Archaeologists have found canoes in Florida that are 5,000 years old! The native people used fire to burn and soften the wood of a pine log. Then they chipped out the burned parts to make a space for people to sit. Dugouts allowed Archaic people to canoe the rivers and coasts all over Florida, saving time because canoeing is much faster than swimming or walking. Still, long before the Archaic people made these discoveries, the Paleo-Indians survived without pottery, canoes, or even spear-throwers. How did they do this? Keep reading to find out.

3

Tenerife's Tales

New characters in this section:

Ashefa (Uh-SHE-fuh): A forty-four-year-old Timucua woman married to Tenerife

Emisu (Eh-MEE-soo): An eleven-year-old Timucua boy, Kidawe's older brother

Hassalla (Ha-SAH-la): A fourteen-year-old Paleo-Indian boy on his first mammoth hunt

Kateema (Ka-TEE-ma): A young, pregnant Timucua woman, the daughter of Sheko

Kidawe (Kee-DA-weh): A five-year-old Timucua boy, Emisu's younger brother

Old Tenerife (Te-ne-REE-fe): A forty-three-year-old Timucua man married to Ashefa

Chief Saturiwa (Sa-chur-EE-wa): Chief of thirty Timucua villages on the east side of the St. Johns River

A low humming wind blew through the council house, licking up flames in the **hearth** fire. Old Tenerife held the bearskin curtain aside as his wife ducked out through the low doorway. He watched Ashefa walk toward the birthing hut. The women's soft chanting grew louder as she opened the door flap and stepped inside. Kateema's baby was coming early, and the **shaman** was away with the men on a hunt. All of the women were helping Kateema, chanting their encouragement and hope. Ashefa had helped with many births. The other women would look to her for guidance. Tenerife looked down at his old and weathered hands. He didn't feel like going home to an empty hut.

Wind whipped long strands of Tenerife's black hair as he tied the heavy bearskin across the doorway. Inside, he rubbed his chilled arms and legs then stepped back toward the fire's warmth. Goose bumps rippled his skin and twisted his many tattoos. He rubbed his arms harder and shivered. Even during the summer **moon**, he was always cold. Tenerife had only lived through forty-three winters. He was too young to have a body this worn out.

Tenerife rubbed his right hip, feeling the large bullet-shaped dent in his skin. It marked the beginning of a great journey, and the beginning of his old age. Tenerife had worn that scar for more than thirty winters. He had lived through many hard seasons, but this was the hardest. For the first time, he had watched the other men jog off on a hunt, instead of going with them. He tried to rub the ache out of his hip. It wasn't fair, he thought. He should be hunting for at least a few more winters. He wasn't that old yet, but he might as well be. He was too old to hunt.

Tenerife stared into the flames. Ashefa was always telling him he was only old if he acted that way. But that wasn't true. People never asked for his guidance anymore and never showed their respect by calling him "Anacotima"—advisor to the chief. Instead, they called him "Old Tenerife." That's who he was now.

"Tenerife!"

He looked up to see Emisu pushing through the opening in the bearskin door. The eleven-winters boy pulled his younger brother in behind him.

"What's wrong, Emisu?" Tenerife asked.

"Kidawe won't stop crying. He's afraid of the wind. Father and

Fig. E. Old Tenerife

Uncle are still away on the hunt, and Mother's in the women's hut helping Kateema have her baby. Can you tell him a story or something? He's been crying ever since it got dark."

"I want my mother," Kidawe mumbled.

"I told you," Emisu said. "She's in the women's hut with Kateema!"

"I want my mother." Kidawe's voice got louder with each word. "I want my mother!"

Tenerife watched the boy pull away and run toward the doorway. "Kidawe!" he called. "I have something for you. Do you want to wear it for luck?"

The five-winters boy turned around. "What is it?"

Tenerife pulled a leather necklace over his head. A shiny gray spear point hung on it. "It belongs to Ashefa," he said. "A point made by the Ancient People. You can wear it during the storm. It will keep you safe."

"Really?" Kidawe shrugged the tears off his face and walked toward the older man. Tenerife motioned him to lean forward, then looped the leather strip around Kidawe's neck. The boy gripped the stone point, measuring it against the length of his hand. The point was longer. "Who made this?" he asked.

Tenerife relaxed back on his leaning bench. In seasons past, hundreds of people had filled the council house to hear his tales. He looked around the large empty hut. It didn't matter. If these boys needed a tale, he would give them one. Lightning flashed above the smoke hole, and Tenerife waited for the thunder to end. When it was quiet enough to hear the soft chanting from the women's hut, Tenerife began. His words were low and melodic, leading the boys back to an ancient world.

Hassalla crouched low in the tall marsh grasses, the needle-sharp reeds poking him in a hundred spots. Each tiny poke itched terribly, and the gnats biting his arms and back were even worse. But he ignored them all. It was the morning of his first ***mammoth*** *hunt, the day he would earn his tattoos and become a man.*

Hassalla's nose twitched. Was it time? Yes, there it was—the smell of smoke. The men had started the fire. Hassalla longed to stand up and look for the far-off blaze, but he stayed crouched and hidden. He had the most important job of the hunt—turning the mammoths toward the trap. If he failed, the tribe would lose their last chance to hunt the great beasts before the next winter moon.

Hassalla shifted the carrier on his back. It held four ***cane*** *spears tipped with dark stone points. He pulled out his favorite spear and tested its sharpness on a piece of his long black hair. It was a point worthy of a mammoth hunt.*

The wind shifted, and Hassalla tasted more smoke in the air. He listened for his prey, trying to hear beyond the breezy rustling of the marsh

Fig. F. Columbian mammoth

grasses and the sound of his own breathing. There. He could just hear the mammoths.

No, he could feel them. There was a slight trembling of the ground, the shaking of the earth caused by a herd of mammoth running at full speed.

They were coming.

4

Fire Drive

Hassalla pressed his palm to the muddy earth to feel its trembling. The mammoths were still far away, but not for long. He unwrapped a piece of mammoth tusk from his hip pack. It held a tiny glowing **ember** for lighting his torches. Each torch was more than three **footsteps** long, made of tightly tied marsh grasses. The **shaman** had worn his mammoth mask and chanted words of magic to bless each torch, bringing luck to the hunt.

As the shaman had instructed, Hassalla closed his eyes and asked the spirit of the mammoth for permission to hunt his mammoth children. He promised to use the mammoth's body to provide food and tools and shelter for the Marsh People. When Hassalla opened his eyes, he felt the sting of smoke. The mammoths were coming.

Hassalla had seen mammoths all of his life, for nearly fifteen winters. He had cut through thick mammoth hides and scraped them clean to make hut coverings and twisted long mammoth fur into rope. He had even helped crack large mammoth bones so the women could scrape out the **marrow** for food. And after all the work, he had feasted on juicy mammoth steaks marbled with rich fat. Hassalla had spent his whole life around mammoths, but he had never seen a live one up close.

He felt the ground tremble more beneath his knees and feet, but it was not time yet. His father had said not to light the torches until he could feel the trembling of the ground in his teeth. He would wait.

Hassalla's eyes stung, and he could taste the smoky air in his mouth. The acrid smell of frightened animals made him wrinkle his nose. Then the breeze turned and carried the mammoth smell away. The animals could probably smell him now—a lone boy crouched in the marsh grasses, waiting to get trampled by a herd of mammoths. Maybe they could smell his fear too. Hassalla concentrated on the trembling of the earth. His elbows and the base of his spine tingled with the vibration, but he could not feel it in his teeth yet. He would wait.

A sudden breeze carried the biting gnats away. The ground continued to tremble, and Hassalla could hear the dull thudding roar of the mammoth's trampling feet. The sharp needle-like marsh grasses whipped furiously, poking Hassalla anew. He rubbed the sting from his arms and felt the jolting of the earth in his shoulders. Tiny splashes jumped in the muddy water around him.

Hassalla swallowed hard. He had to time this just right. The mammoths were running in terror now, fleeing the approaching fire. His job was to turn the herd toward a deep spot in the marsh. Most of the mammoths would crash on through the deep spot and escape on the other side. But some, the older ones or the inexperienced young ones, would get ***mired*** *in the thick black marsh mud. His tribe's hunters would be ready for them.*

But the mammoths knew about the dangers of the deep spot. They would never go there willingly. They would head toward the shallow area, right behind Hassalla. And it was up to Hassalla to stop them with a smoky fire of his own. If he lit his torches too early, the mammoths would see the trap and escape. If he lit them too late, the mammoths would run right over him. He had to light them at just the right moment—late enough so the mammoths couldn't avoid the trap, but soon enough to give them time to veer toward the deep marsh. Mammoths, like other animals, were terrified of smoke and flame. If

Fig. G. Hassalla on the hunt

Hassalla could frighten the lead mammoth into turning, all the others would follow. If he could get them to turn.

Hassalla looked around. There were a few stunted bushes, but no trees to climb if he failed. He blinked his eyes against the stinging smoke. For the first time, he felt the searing heat of the wall of flame moving toward him. If all went well, the deep water of the marsh would stop the approaching flames. The fire would die quickly, and the men could attack the mired mammoths. Hassalla took a deep breath. The trembling of the earth had moved into his teeth and nose. It was time.

Carefully, he lit each torch from the ember he carried in the tip of the mammoth's tusk. With four torches in his hands and four spears lashed to his back, he held his breath and listened. He could just hear the shouts of the men of his tribe herding the mammoths toward the marsh—and toward him.

The strong scent of frightened mammoths filled Hassalla's nostrils. He stood up slowly, torches ready. The mammoths were still far away, but he could see the giant animals hurtling toward him. The front mammoth was at least thirteen footsteps tall. Hassalla thought of his own height of less than six footsteps and swallowed hard. He felt his chest thumping wildly and wanted to run—anywhere away from the mammoths. What good was being a man if you were squashed flat by a herd of mammoths? The huge animals were pounding toward him at top speed, trumpeting their anger and fear. But Hassalla didn't run. He was too scared to move. He held his torches ready.

Thunder pounded the air, interrupting Tenerife's story. Both Emisu and Kidawe jumped at the loud sound. More thunder rumbled around the council house. Tenerife wove the frightening sound into his story and continued the tale.

That rumbling is just what Hassalla heard. But he stood his ground as a living storm of flesh and fur hurtled toward him. Hassalla could feel beads of sweat forming on his forehead and dripping into his eyes. He held his torches low to keep the smoke from traveling to the mammoths too soon. Luck was with him. The wind blew powerfully toward him, carrying the smoke away from the terrified herd.

The mammoths pounded closer and closer at top speed. Hassalla's whole body trembled with the shaking earth. He listened to the mammoths' trumpeting as they thundered towards him, trying to escape the small shouting humans and the terrifying flames.

There were fourteen mammoths in all. The one in front was grayish brown, with much of its thick winter coat hanging in tangled knots. There were five females, some with young, and several old mammoths with large curved tusks. But it was the one in front that Hassalla watched. He had to turn that mammoth. His life depended on it.

Hassalla wanted to leap out and wave his torches—anything to make the mammoths go away. But his people needed the meat and hides this hunt would provide. So he waited, even though his chest squeezed up tight, and he felt like he couldn't breathe.

Finally, something inside him said, "Now!" Hassalla leaped forward, waving the flaming torches wildly at the stampeding mammoths. He shouted and jumped up and down. The wind whipped his glowing torches into flames three footsteps long. Armed with the frightening flames, he ran straight toward the herd. At his signal, ten other men leaped out of the grasses. Each shouted from a different spot along the shallow marsh, intent on turning the mammoths toward the deeper waters.

But the mammoths were not turning. Hassalla ran straight toward them, waving his torches and shouting at the top of his lungs. The mammoth herd was only a hundred footsteps away. Hassalla could see the lead mammoth's face as it charged toward him. Its black eyes watered in the smoky air and looked about wildly through the fire and noise. Suddenly, the mammoth lowered its tusks and dropped into a dead gallop—right at Hassalla.

5

Mammoth Hunt

"What did Hassalla do?" Kidawe asked.

"The only thing he could do," Tenerife said.

Hassalla stood his ground, waving and shouting like the others. He could feel the heat of the approaching fire deep in his muscles. Then, suddenly, the skin on his back cooled. The wind had shifted again, blowing toward the herd.

The lead mammoth slowed, sampling the air with its trunk. Moments later, it veered left, taking the herd with it.

"The smoke," Hassalla yelled, "they've just now smelled our smoke!" He coughed and waved his torches harder. The herd was only thirty footsteps away when the last mammoth turned. Hassalla and the men chased after them with the other hunters, waving their torches and shouting as loud as they could.

Hassalla ran until he thought his chest would burst. He couldn't have stopped if he wanted to. The wall of fire was right behind him. He had to make it to the far side of the deep marsh to be safe. Hassalla's leg muscles trembled with fatigue, but still he pushed on. Finally, he was there. Two mammoths had sunk up to their knees and were trying to escape. The rest of the herd had floundered on through. It was the two in the trap that mattered.

Hassalla could feel the fire's heat as it burned closer to the sprinting hunters. The flames shone brightly in the dark waters of the salt marsh as he splashed through to the other side, safe.

The men howled like wolves and ran toward the mired mammoths. Some were already thrusting their spears at the large beasts. Each hunter aimed for a vital spot, trying to kill the mammoths quickly and end their suffering.

The marsh was filled with shouting, struggling motion. Men were running and shouting and thrusting spears with deadly accuracy. The two mammoths swung their trunks and dangerous tusks at hunters that came too close, trumpeting their anger and fear at the small hunters. Hassalla tried hard to block out all the noise and heat and motion. He splashed cool marsh water over his face and back, then took four deep breaths to steady himself. He was ready.

Hassalla chose a hunting spot near the younger mammoth, a male with short tusks and reddish-brown fur. Only ten footsteps away, it towered over the human hunters. Hassalla could smell the mammoth's fear and blood in the air. The animal swung its powerful trunk toward the hunters, and Hassalla fought the urge to step back.

He darted forward and thrust his first spear at one of the mammoth's eyes. But the beast turned its head at the last moment, and the spear only grazed its ear harmlessly.

The eye was too small a target, he thought. The belly was easier. It would cause a slower death, but with the spears of the other hunters, a belly wound could take the beast down. Hassalla carefully aimed his second spear and lunged forward to attack. His spear stuck tight in the mammoth's belly, and the beast slashed angrily at the closest hunters.

Hassalla leaped away from the sharp tusks. Several hunters stumbled back, while others moved in closer. One of the younger men staggered past Hassalla, pressing his hand to a bloody gash in his right leg. Hassalla moved to help him, but the young man waved him back to the hunt.

Hassalla gripped his third spear tightly. The ribs, he thought. His father had told him a spear between the ribs could pierce a lung and end the beast's suffering. It wasn't easy to hit the narrow spaces between the ribs though, and Hassalla only had two spears left. But he would try. He dashed up to the beast's ribcage and slammed his spear into the tough hide. It stuck in, but not very far. The point must have hit a bony rib instead of going between them. "No!" He dodged away from the flailing spear as the mammoth whipped around.

He had to make this last spear count. Hassalla tried to ignore the splashing and calling of the hunters and mammoths around him. He watched the movement of the mammoth's ribs as it took great labored breaths. There, he thought, choosing his target. Between those ribs. He waited for a spot among the men to clear and then dashed up to the mammoth. His strike was quick and clean, and his spear sliced between the mammoth's ribs. The great beast coughed and sputtered, then sagged sideways in the muddy water. A moment later, the other mammoth, an old female with long curved tusks, trumpeted a last call and fell beside the male.

The air was perfectly quiet.

Then it was filled with the wolf-like howls and excited shouts of the hunters. The men jumped up and down and splashed each other with marsh water. Hassalla sat still amid the tall marsh grasses. He felt weak, all his energy spent on the hunt. But the other hunters were laughing and calling to him. Somehow, he found his strength and walked to the fallen mammoths. The tribe's leader joined him.

"Hassalla has become a man today!" The leader held Hassalla's arms up for all to see. "Find your spears."

Each hunter of the tribe put special markings on the cane shafts of his spears. Hassalla only found two of his, the one in the mammoth's belly and the one that went between its ribs. He pulled them out carefully, hoping to save their stone points. The one from the animal's belly came out whole, but the one from its ribs was broken lengthwise. It was useless.

The leader spoke to him. "Save that broken point, Hassalla. Give it to your sons to remind them that you made the kill on your first mammoth hunt." Hassalla nodded and rinsed the broken point in the marsh water. The other men divided the mammoths' livers and gave a piece to each hunter. The raw liver tasted warm and salty in his mouth.

Hassalla walked over and laid his hands on the tusks of the male mammoth. He spoke to its spirit, thanking the great beast for its sacrifice, and promising to use each part of the mammoth for the good of the Marsh People. Then he stood and looked around at the golden green marsh grasses to the east and the singed, trampled ground to the west. He could already see the tribe's women walking toward them. They were preparing to butcher the beasts—to make the food and tools the Marsh People needed to survive. Hassalla took a deep breath of warm smoky air. It was a good day.

As the story ended, Kidawe gripped the old point with small respectful fingers. "This point hunted a giant animal," he whispered. "A mammoth."

"What other animals did they hunt?" Emisu asked.

"The Ancient Ones also hunted turtles as big as bears," Tenerife answered, "and if they were careless, panthers with long spear-like teeth hunted them!"

Kidawe grinned. "How did you learn about the Ancient Marsh People?"

"My grandmother told me that story. She learned it from her

grandfather before her. The tale was passed from person to person ever since the time of the giant animals."

A gust of wind blew in through the smoke hole, spattering them with more cold raindrops. Tenerife wrapped a feather **matchcoat** around his shoulders. It was old and tattered, a gift from Chief Saturiwa long ago, but it still kept the rain off. He handed the boys two soft deer furs, and they wrapped themselves warmly, with the thick fur side close to their skin.

The boys flinched as thunder pounded the air again. The village dogs barked wildly, and the boys pulled their furs close around them. Kidawe gripped the ancient spear point. "Tenerife," he asked, "can you tell us another story?"

Historic Native Peoples

6

Woodland Indians

Florida's Archaic people continued to develop new ideas and new ways of doing things. Bows and arrows were invented, improving hunting accuracy and distance. New skills like pottery-making and gardening encouraged tribes to stay in one place all year instead of moving around. Historians recognize these important changes by giving the native people a new name: Woodland Indians.

Woodland people made many discoveries. They were the first Florida Indians to grow crops in gardens. They even found a better way to make pottery. The old Archaic method mixed palmetto fibers or Spanish moss into wet clay, which made pottery that was thick and heavy. Woodland Indians discovered how to make thin, light pottery by mixing in sand or crushed freshwater sponges instead. (Look back at figure D on page 14 and ahead at figure II on page 136.)

Woodland Indians also carved **ceremonial** items from wood, shell, and copper. They often shaped these religious figures and pictures to look like animals, birdmen, or eyes. Chiefs, shamans, and other native people of high status were sometimes buried with these ceremonial items. Other times, important people were buried with copper ear decorations or sheets of mica. Since copper and mica come from the Appalachian Mountains, not from Florida, archaeologists have evidence that Florida's Woodland Indians were trading with faraway native groups.

Earthworks were another important aspect of Woodland Indian culture. These dirt structures include mounds, canals, and dirt fences. Archaeologists think the people built mounds to show status or importance. The chief's house and the village temple were probably built on top of these impressive 30-foot hills. Earthwork canals connected villages with nearby bodies of water, so canoes could go back and forth. Even though the Archaic Indians invented canoes, Woodland people used canoes much more often. Embankments (long, narrow, artificial hills) may have served as dirt fences to protect ceremonial areas. Because Woodland chiefs could organize workers and supplies for these large earthwork projects, we know that native leaders were getting more powerful.

As Woodland Indians settled into Florida's different environments, they learned to use the natural materials available in each place. For example, the St. Johns people grew corn in rich soils, while the Caloosahatchee people mainly hunted water animals. These Woodland cultures were the great-grandparents of later native groups. The St. Johns culture became the Timucua people, and the Caloosahatchee became the Calusa.

7

Who Were They?

About 500 years ago, the great-grandchildren of Woodland Indians formed the many different native groups in Florida, including the Ais, Apalachee, Calusa, Guacate, Hobe, Jeaga, Jororo, Matecumbe, Mayaca, Santaluces, Tequesta, Timucua, and Tocobago. But who were these historic people? (See figure H.)

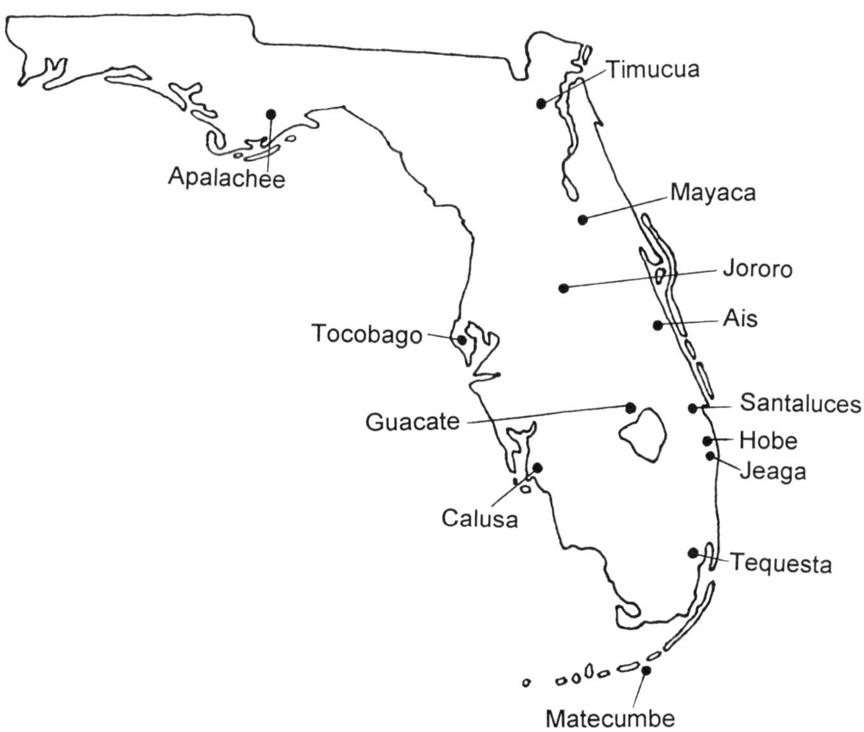

Fig. H. Map of native groups in early Florida

The name "historic" refers to all the Indians who lived in Florida AFTER the Europeans arrived in A.D. 1513. They are called "historic" Indians because the Europeans wrote histories about them. (Before contact with Europeans, Florida's native people did not read or write. Their histories were remembered and told by storytellers.)

The histories written by the Spanish, French, and English teach us much of what we know about Florida's historic Indians. They tell us that native people had light-brown skin and long dark hair. In many cultures, historic people only cut their hair to show sadness. The men wore their hair long or tied into a knot or

Fig. I. Florida's early native people

ponytail. They sometimes decorated it with foxtails or egret feathers. These people were about the same height as people in Florida today—5½ to 6 feet tall. (See figure I.)

Men and women both wore ear pins or ear spools made from shell, bone, pearls, or fish bladders. They also wore beads and jangles, jewelry that jingled when they walked. The men and women wore leather loincloths that looked like today's bikini bathing suits. Some women also wore a skirt or sash made of moss cloth, woven bark, or animal skin. Florida Indians knew how to make moccasins, but they usually did not wear them. They also made **matchcoats**. These big wrap-around coats were made from **leather** for warmth or from weatherproof feathers to block the rain. (Look back at Figure E on page 18.)

Many native groups decorated their skin with tattoos. They poked their skin with a bone needle to make dotted designs and then rubbed **ashes** or berry juice into the holes. The more tattoos a person had, the more important he or she was in the village. Chiefs had more tattoos than anyone else.

Other native groups used body paint instead of tattoos. Body paint could show what ball team a person was on, whether he was heading to battle, or how important he was. Many native chiefs and shamans had special body paint to show their **status**.

Native kids probably woke up before the sun rose and went to bed at sunset. They practiced adult skills, such as making tools, scraping animal hides, and gathering wild plants. They also competed in races to build up their speed. Forest games of hide-and-go-seek taught them to be excellent trackers, and ball games or spear-throwing games helped them become skilled hunters and warriors. They also had swimming, canoeing, and fishing contests to develop good water skills. Children and adult

Fig. J. French **engraving** of Timucua games, by Theodore de Bry

hunters all competed in these games to sharpen their skills and find out who was the best. (See figure J.)

When grandmothers and grandfathers were too old to hunt or work in the fields, they took on new jobs, like scaring animals away from the gardens and watching for thieves. They cared for small children and taught them hunting and weaving skills. They also told stories and advised the chief.

When Florida's historic Indians died, they were buried in a **burial mound**. People with higher status were often buried with special items like shell bowls, pottery, or copper ear pins. Sometimes people were buried right after they died, in a ceremony called a primary burial. Other times, dead people were

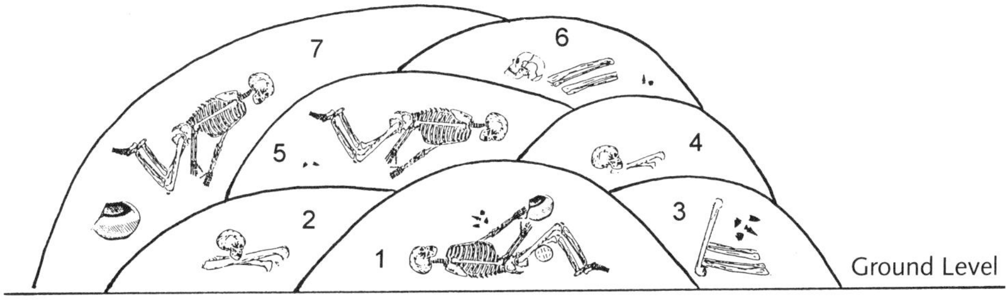

Dirt is piled up over the skeleton each time someone is buried. Can you see how the mound shape is formed? Number 1 was buried first, then 2, then 3, and so on.

Fig. K. How a burial mound is formed

kept in a **charnel house** until they were mostly bones. Then the bones were tied into a bundle and buried in the mound. These were called bundle burials. (See figure K.) These special burial methods suggest that Florida Indians believed in a spirit world or afterlife.

8

Living Near the Water

Because all people need water for drinking, bathing, and cooking, native villages were always located near water. People who lived near a river got drinking water from the river. Groups with homes near a salty **marsh** or an ocean had to look for springs to drink from. A spring is a place where fresh underground water bubbles up through the soil. Florida has many springs. You can visit one called Silver Springs in Ocala. (The city of Ocala is named after a Timucua Indian group—the Ocale people.)

All Florida Indians got some of their food from the water. They collected shellfish, such as oysters, snails, whelks, clams, and mussels. They also ate reptiles and **amphibians** and their eggs, including alligators, water snakes, sea turtles, freshwater turtles, turtle eggs, and frogs. Water birds and their eggs were also on the menu. These included ducks, geese, pelicans, and egrets. Florida Indians also ate water mammals, including dolphins, manatees, otters, pilot whales, and seals. (Caribbean monk seals once lived in Florida's waters, but they are extinct today.) Native people ate plenty of crustaceans, like crabs, shrimp, lobster, and crayfish. And, of course, they ate freshwater and saltwater fish, including bass, catfish, drum, gar, mullet, shark, and trout. (Look ahead at figure BB on page 100.) They used many fishing methods, including nets, **weirs**, **gigs**, traps, spears, and hooks and lines, but no fishing poles. (Look ahead at figure V on page 75.)

In addition to hunting water animals, native people also harvested **wetland** plants. Glasswort plants added a salty flavor to foods, and sea grapes grew wild on south Florida beaches. Native people used river **cane** for arrow **shafts**, cordgrass for weaving, and cypress trees for canoes. Their **dugouts** were much longer than modern canoes, and some could hold 10–20 standing men.

Native men prepared for a hunt or a battle by participating in a **cassina** (or black drink) ceremony. They drank this hot

Fig. L. French engraving of a cassina ceremony, by Theodore de Bry

caffeinated tea to get energy and good luck, but it sometimes made them vomit. Different native groups had differing ideas about this physical reaction. In some cases, throwing up meant a person was weak and had to miss the hunt. Other times, vomiting meant a person had **purified** his body and was ready to go. (See figure L, which shows some Timucua men throwing up.) In historic cultures, men did most of the hunting, but women hunted too, especially for smaller animals. Women also made the cassina, but only men were allowed to drink it. To make cassina, native women collected yaupon holly leaves from coastal, marshy areas.

Most of Florida's native villages were located near salt marshes, rivers, or oceans. This gave native people easy access to yaupon holly plants and the other natural resources discussed in this chapter. While these people depended on the water, they also needed land resources. Keep reading to find out why.

9

Foods and Tools

Florida's Indians hunted many land animals. They looked for reptiles such as snakes and tortoises, as well as birds like quail, dove, and turkey. They also hunted mammals, including deer, foxes, mice, opossums, pigs that had escaped from the Spanish, rabbits, raccoons, squirrels, and wolves. (Long ago, there were many red wolves in Florida, but today they are nearly extinct.)

Native people got more than meat from these animals. They used animal hides to make warm furs and leather. Stomachs and bladders were made into canteens, fat into medicines, and **tendons** into thread. (Tendons are the stringy connectors that hook muscle to bone.) Native people also used bones and antlers to make hammers, fishhooks, flutes, knives, needles, and whistles. They wasted nothing. Since Florida had no hard metal and very little stone, they often used seashells to make bowls, ear pins, hoes, axes, net weights, and scrapers. (See figure M.)

Tools like shell hoes were very useful in villages that planted gardens. (Look ahead at figure NN on page 157). While men usually cleared the fields, the women planted and harvested the crops. Each family might also have a small garden next to its hut, where the family grew its favorite plants and herbs.

They planted some sunflowers but their four main crops

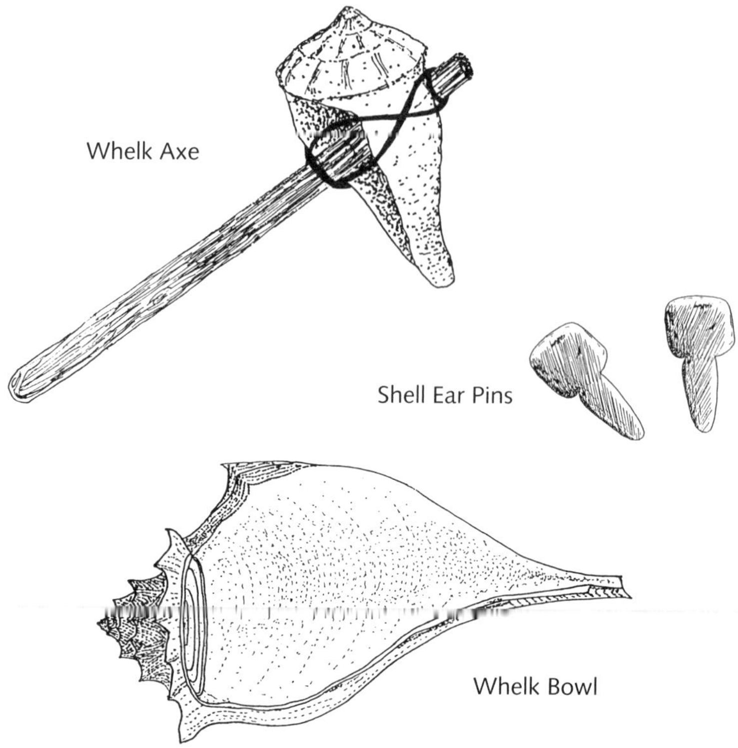

Fig. M. Shell tools used by Florida Indians

were corn, beans, squash, and pumpkins. Farming villages planted corn twice each year, in early spring and again in midsummer. During very dry times, native people may have carried water out to their crops in gourd buckets.

After the harvest, the native people set aside plenty of beans, seeds, and kernels to use in the next planting. The rest were used as food. Woodland people ate some corn fresh from the stalk and dried the rest in the sun. Later, they soaked the dried corn to make soft, puffy **hominy**. They also pounded dried corn into grits or into flour to make cornbread. They ate sunflower seeds raw and also boiled them for their oil. Corn, beans, pumpkins, squashes, and their seeds could be eaten raw or cooked. Because gourds were too hard to eat, native people dried them out, removed their seeds, and used the hollow woody shapes as bowls, scoops, buckets, or birdhouses. Florida Indians also planted tobacco for use in some ceremonies. They did not know that smoking tobacco caused cancer. (See figure N.)

Only some of Florida's Indians planted gardens. However, they all gathered food plants from the woods. They collected fruits like blackberries, blueberries, grapes, persimmons, and

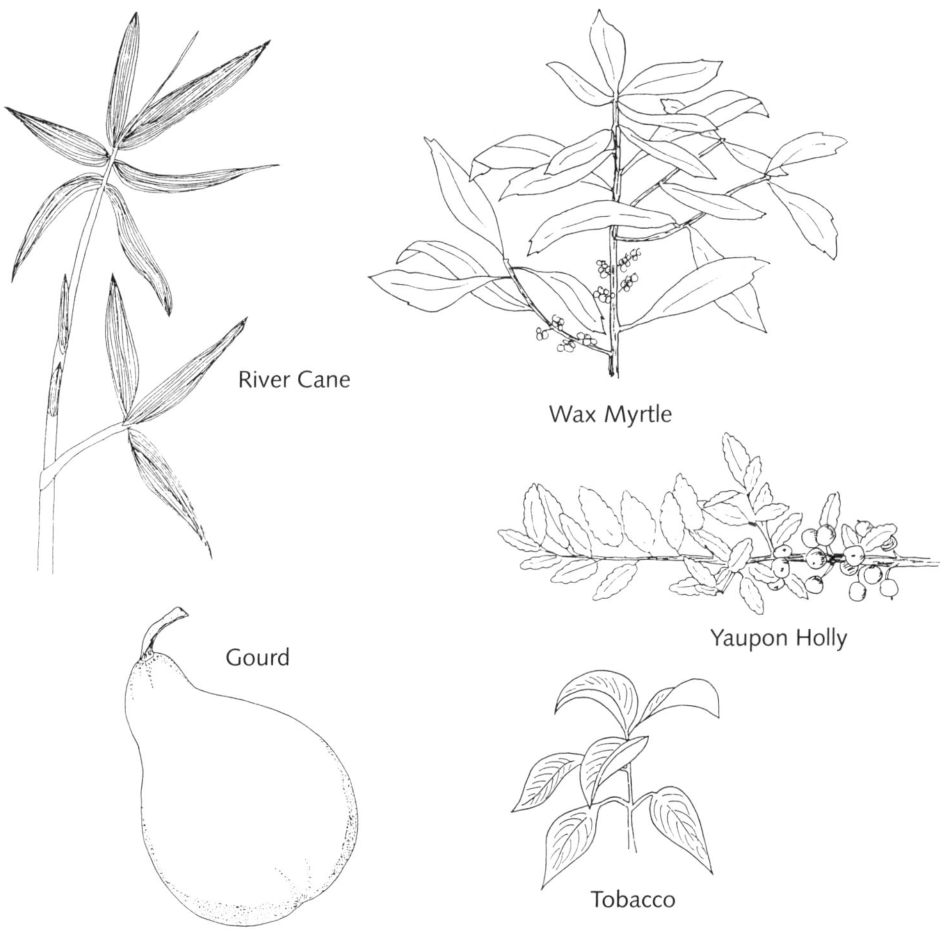

Fig. N. Plants used by Florida Indians. Wax myrtle leaves were used to make insect repellent. Gourds were made into bowls and dippers. Tobacco leaves were used in ceremonies. River cane stems were made into arrows. Yaupon holly leaves were roasted and boiled to make the black drink, cassina.

plums. They ground up acorns, cattail roots, or pigweed seeds to make flour and breads. Bay leaves, onions, and peppergrass seeds added spice to their food, while chinquapin and hickory nuts provided rich, tasty oils. Thistle and pokeweed leaves were eaten as greens. Maple sap was boiled to make syrup and candy, while sweetgum sap was chewed as gum.

Florida Indians also used plants to make tools. They made cypress and pine canoes, gourd bowls, grapevine baskets, river cane arrows, palm huts, and moss cloth. Other tools were made from stone and clay. **Chert**, a whitish-gray stone, was made into hoes, drills, and scrapers, as well as projectile points like knives, arrowheads, and spearheads. (Look back at figure C on page 12.) Each stone tool started out as a chunk of rock. Native toolmakers used antler hammers to knock off large chips of stone. This made the basic tool shape. Then they used the tip of an antler to press off tiny, delicate chips. This gave their stone tools sharp cutting edges. Projectile points made from wood, bone, and stingray spines were also sharp and effective.

Clay, another natural resource found in Florida, was used to make pottery. The native people mixed this slimy soil with water and sometimes sand. Then they rolled the clay into long ropes, coiled them into a pot shape, and hardened the pot in a fire. This **coiled pottery** was light and strong. (Look ahead at figure Y on page 84 to see how pottery was coiled.)

Pottery, tools, and gardens were just a few of the land resources used by Florida's Indians. They also needed space to make their homes. Keep reading to learn about Florida's early homes and villages.

10

Homes and Villages

Florida Indians did *not* live in tepees. Tepees were usually made of buffalo skins, but there weren't many buffalo in Florida. Instead, Florida's Indians built huts made of wooden poles and palm fronds. Each family had its own hut that was about 20 feet across. Some native people built circular houses, while others built rectangular ones. Each hut had a low doorway and a hole in the palm roof to let smoke escape. Along the inside walls of the hut, benches provided space for sleeping and sitting. Personal tools and toys were hung on the inside of the hut walls. These palm walls did not keep bugs out, so Florida Indians built **smudge** fires under their sleeping benches. These small corncob fires didn't make much flame, but their smoke kept bugs away from the people while they slept.

Most huts had a big fire pit near the center. The family could cook there, but they probably did most of their cooking outside at community fire pits. Except for sleeping, most family activities occurred outside the hut.

In some villages, each family had two huts, one for winter and one for summer. The winter hut had a roof and walls of tightly **thatched** palm fronds to keep the family warm on cold nights. (See figure O.) The summer hut had a thick roof of palms to block the rain, but the sides were open to let in breezes. The chief's house was probably larger than other homes. Sometimes it was built on top of a tall hill made of dirt or shells.

In some native villages, the huts were clustered together. Ten to fifty family huts may have surrounded a huge council house big enough to seat everyone in the village. This council house had room for storytelling and dancing, tool-making, and meetings. While some French drawings show rectangular council houses in Florida, archaeologists believe that many Florida council houses were actually circular. (Look at the rectangular

Fig. O. An early native hut with a palm-thatched roof. Compare this to the Seminole chickee hut in figure VV on page 185.

Fig. P. French engraving of a native village, by Theodore de Bry

council house in the center of figure P. Then look ahead at figure JJ on page 138 to see a circular council house.)

Did you also notice the guard shack and the village fence in figure P? Some Florida Indians may have used a protective palisade or fence, but most did not. Other villages had guard shacks with spy holes so hunters could watch for strangers or shoot at enemies.

In some parts of Florida, family groups built their huts a few miles from the nearest council house. This allowed them to live close to their gardens. These families traveled to the council house for meetings, ceremonies, dancing, and storytelling. For them, the council house was like the capital of a spread-out farming community. Keep reading to visit a Timucua council house.

11

The Storm

New characters in this section:

Atore (Ah-TOR-eh): A teenage Timucua boy, nephew and heir to Chief Saturiwa

Leena (LEE-na): A five-year-old Timucua girl, Simaru's sister

Simaru (Si-MA-roo): An eleven-year-old Timucua boy, Leena's older brother and Emisu and Kidawe's cousin

Young Saturiwa (Sa-chur-EE-wa): A fourteen-year-old bully, the nephew of a chief

A chill wind whipped in through the council house door, bringing up goose bumps on Tenerife's arms and legs. Emisu and Kidawe looked out at the storm and asked again, "Can you tell us another story?"

Tenerife nodded and pushed blowing strands of black hair behind his ears. He watched Emisu grip his younger brother's shoulders.

"Come on, Kidawe," the older boy said. "Don't be scared. You've got the ancient spear point. Besides, Chief Saturiwa wouldn't be afraid. Don't you want to be brave like him? Tell him, Tenerife. Wasn't Chief Saturiwa brave and smart—even when he was little?"

Tenerife thought a moment. "Saturiwa wasn't always so brave and smart."

Slowly, Kidawe looked up at him. "He wasn't?"

Emisu looked over at Tenerife. "What do you mean?"

"I said Chief Saturiwa wasn't always brave and smart." He hadn't told this story for many winters. All of the adults remembered it, but it wasn't one of Chief Saturiwa's favorite stories.

For a moment, Tenerife could hear the women's chanting rise above the humming wind. He took a deep breath and began.

There was a time, long ago, when Saturiwa had only lived through fourteen winters. He was tall and strong, but not yet wise.

"What happened?" Kidawe asked. The five-winters boy leaned forward. "What was Saturiwa like?"

"He and I were both boys then, Kidawe. I was much like Emisu here, not the biggest boy, but perhaps one of the smartest. Chief Saturiwa was much like his nephew, Atore."

"Just what we need," Emisu said, "another Atore."

Tenerife knew what those two boys thought of each other. It would take time to get past those feelings. Perhaps the story would help. He waited for the rumbling thunder to end, then began his story.

It was the blueberry moon, Tenerife said, my turn to empty the fishing weir. And I had come up with a plan, maybe the cleverest plan of my whole life.

"What was it?" Kidawe blurted out.

Note: A weir is a fish trap made of fences. These fences direct fish to swim toward an enclosed space. When the tide goes out, the water level drops, trapping the fish within this space. (Look ahead at figure Q on page 52 to see an example of a weir.)

Emisu elbowed his younger brother. "Let him tell it!"

Tenerife grinned and continued.

It was a warm day, with little breeze. I was chest-deep in salt water, halfway down the middle of the southern fishing weir, almost to the barrier. The water was rising with the ***tide****. It was time to put my plan into action. A few slogging steps ahead, the cane barrier blocked my path. It stuck just above the water's surface. I slung my bladder canteen across my back and hooked one leg over the barrier. Saturiwa was always calling me a shrimp, saying how they should boil me up someday. Well, I knew I wasn't the tallest eleven-winters boy, but Saturiwa was never going to boil me.*

Fig. Q. Young Tenerife in the weir

"Chief Saturiwa called you a shrimp?" Emisu shouted. "But you're Anacotima, one of his Noble Men!"

Kidawe elbowed his older brother. "Be quiet, remember?" Emisu elbowed him back.

Tenerife ignored the boys. He was listening to the storm. The constant humming wind was changing to a ripping sound. Palm fronds were being stripped from the roof. Tenerife scanned the inside of the palm ceiling—no torn spots. He wasn't surprised. The roof was thatched in tight layers. It was made to stand up to rough weather. Still, winds like these made everyone nervous. It would be a long night. Tenerife looked down at the boys. Kidawe was staring at the roof, gripping the ancient point tightly. Emisu was stoking the hearth fire with a stick, but every few moments, he looked up toward the windy smoke hole.

Tenerife followed the boys' gaze. He watched the fire's smoke whip around in shaky circles, then disappear through the hole above. There was little danger here. The village huts were strong enough for winds like these. Besides, a good storytelling could break a storm's power.

"Anacotima," Kidawe whispered. "Is it **Huque**?"

"No, child," Tenerife said. "It is not Huque. I have lived through many of the great storms, so I watch for the signs. It is not Huque."

Kidawe nodded his head. "Thank you for your wisdom, Anacotima."

Tenerife breathed in deeply. Those formal words sounded strange on such a young tongue. Anacotima. No one had called him that since he'd stopped hunting with the younger men.

It was good to be Anacotima again.

12

The Plan

Quietly, Tenerife began to speak, building the power of his story against the storm.

On that warm day in the blueberry moon, I had decided to teach Saturiwa a lesson. I grabbed hold of the weir's barrier poles and scooted over the top. My first foot down brushed a captured fish. I was supposed to have gathered the fish earlier that afternoon, when the tide was lower. But I had been busy. It was all part of my plan.

It was a hunt day. All the boys had drawn lots to see who would empty the fishing weir, and I got stuck with the job. You know the rule. A hunter can't go into a fish trap before a hunt. If he does, he's unclean—bad luck. I decided it was time to put that rule to the test.

I moved to the closed V-end of the trap and wedged myself against the river cane poles. A yellow fly buzzed around my head in the hot still afternoon air. The tide was on its way in, bringing waters that would free the captured fish. Flashes of silver marked the mullet and trout that shared my trap. It seemed like a waste to let them escape. I peeked between the tall cane poles at the oyster shells and fish bones that covered the muddy shoreline. My uncle walked up to empty a basket of trash, and I hid, waiting for him to leave.

I peered at the midden again. It wasn't that far away. Maybe I

Fig. R. Taking trash to the midden. Drawing by Merald Clark, from *New Worlds, Old Songs: Understanding the Lives of Ancient Peoples in Southwest Florida through Archaeology,* by Charles E. Blanchard (Gainesville: IAPS Books, 1995).

could throw the fish to the shore. It would be a waste to let them go. I caught a fish on my third grab and flung it over the fence. Quickly, I pressed my face to the cane poles to see if it hit the shore.

"Did you make it?" Kidawe asked. The five-winters boy didn't seem to hear the winds tugging roughly at the palm frond roof.

"No, I didn't," Tenerife said. "I saw the fish splash in the shallows and swim away."

"Oh."

"I wasn't happy either, Kidawe. I thought maybe Saturiwa was right. Maybe I was just a shrimp. But then I got angry. I was an eleven-winters boy, not a full-grown man. Saturiwa was supposed to be bigger than me. He was three winters older. And he got away with picking on everyone just because he was the chief's nephew. He even got the older boys to call me 'Shrimparife of the Shrimp Clan.'"

Emisu laughed out loud.

Then his eyes opened wide and he covered his mouth. "I'm sorry, Anacotima. It's just that Atore treats us the same way."

"I told you Chief Saturiwa was very much like his nephew. I hope Atore gains the wisdom his uncle did. But it took time. And I was one eleven-winters boy who didn't want to wait."

I peeked through the weir fence again and slapped at yellow flies that buzzed around my head. At the V-end of the fish trap, the weir's poles blocked every bit of breeze. There was no wind to blow the bugs away. I ducked underwater to escape the biting flies. As I came back up, I slid my hands along the sturdy poles of the weir. I had helped build that weir the season before, tying the long cane poles together, and helping the grownups force them deep into the muddy creek bottom.

"The south weir?" Emisu asked. "I replaced some poles over there a few moons ago. I didn't know it was thirty winters old!"

"We worked hard to make it strong, Emisu. But weirs take a lot of effort. Every season, we have to replace rotted sections of fence. I wonder if any of the poles I put there are still in place." Tenerife thought of the damage done six winters ago when Huque blew through. He paused to listen to the winds outside but said nothing.

Emisu spoke up. "Simaru and I did the fishing weir a few days ago. We had a good day—about twenty fish. Which parts did you build?"

"I was the oldest boy in the fish **clan**, so I was in charge of the other children working on the trap. We spent days tying cane poles together. But we never imagined our weir would last this long. It was hard enough just getting through the job."

"How come?" Kidawe asked. "I've tied poles. It's not so hard."

"It wasn't the work that was hard. It was Saturiwa. He was cutting poles with the bigger boys, but every time he went by, he yelled something like 'Shrimparife, the baby shrimps are slowing us down. Maybe we should boil you up!' Then he would yank someone's hair. Always someone five or ten winters younger."

"That sounds familiar," Emisu grumbled.

Tenerife paused his story. "More trouble with Atore?" Tenerife asked.

"I don't want to talk about it," Emisu said. "He's a dung ball."

Tenerife tried not to smile. "But he's also the nephew of a chief, Emisu."

"I know, Anacotima. He'll be a chief someday. But he's still a dung ball."

Tenerife nodded. Saturiwa had gained much wisdom, but not enough to share that wisdom with his nephew and heir.

"What happened next?" Emisu asked. "What was the plan?"

It wasn't quite time to spring the trap. While I waited, I slapped at the biting flies around my shoulders. I hadn't had a chance to clean out my bag of wax myrtle lotion since Saturiwa ruined it. So I squatted underwater and scooped a handful of mud from the creek bottom. I wiped the cool wet mud across my shoulders and patted some on my face and neck. I was planning to be there for a while, so there was no sense getting eaten up by flies. If I was right, Saturiwa would be along soon.

Of course, Saturiwa knew nothing about my plan. He had plans of his own. I have talked to him about that day many times. This is what he remembered.

Saturiwa had taken the shell jangles off his legs and the raccoon tail from his hair. That night, he planned to wear only a loincloth—nothing that could jingle and scare his prey or snag on the sharp marsh grasses. It was his first time leading a hunt with the men. A group of seals had been sighted migrating through the needlerush marsh, and his uncle had told him to lead the hunt. He would be leading the older men! He knew all the boys would be jealous. So he strutted around in front of us, practicing spear-throws, showing off. He even drew seal shapes on all the targets at the practice field—even though none of the other boys were getting to hunt seal.

Saturiwa had worked hard to show his chief and uncle that he was ready to lead the men. He'd showed his skills as a hunter by learning the wisdom of the red fox. And he'd proved his strength as a leader by demanding the obedience of the younger boys. At least he had tried. "Someday," he thought, "he would be chief—of hunting, fishing, and battle—and then no little shrimps would get away with talking back to him."

Saturiwa was trying not to think about the boys in the village. His mind needed to be on the hunt. He crushed wax-myrtle leaves into a small clay pot of melted fat. The oils inside those leaves kept bugs away.

He would need this wax-myrtle salve during the hunt. It was supposed to be a still night, with no breeze to blow the gnats and flies away. Saturiwa grinned as he stirred the wax-myrtle lotion.

He was thinking of the stunt he'd pulled a ***hand of days*** *before. He'd switched my wax myrtle lotion with a lotion made from maple-sugar. Saturiwa had watched from the shore, laughing. I was slapping so many bugs that I turned my uncle's canoe over, with my uncle in it. As far as Saturiwa was concerned, I'd gotten just what I deserved. He thought I needed a lesson in how to treat a future chief.*

"Anacotima," Emisu said, "how could you stand it? Chief Saturiwa was just as mean to you as Atore is to us."

"Well," Tenerife answered, "I used my head."

I knew men had to be clean and pure to join a hunt. Any dirt or weakness could bring bad luck to the whole hunting party. Saturiwa would be joining the men for a cassina ceremony right before the hunt. If he was too weak to hold down the sacred black drink, he'd be left behind. So he had to do everything he could to make sure he was ready.

Since he had to be completely clean, I knew he'd never settle for a quick wash at the bathing pot. He'd want to get all the way into the water. The tide was coming in, so the nearby spring would already be covered with saltwater. Saturiwa would have to cross the creek to reach a spring above the high-tide line. And that meant he would need his canoe.

Most boys didn't have their own canoe. They borrowed their uncle's canoe or shared one with the other boys. But Saturiwa had his own. It was boy-sized, small compared to the adult boats that held fifteen men. But it was all his. Still he wasn't satisfied. He was always trying to get the rest of us to build him an adult-sized canoe. But we knew who would end up paddling it—us. So we made excuses. He couldn't make us do the work. But he always tried, and he was always making plans. In fact, Saturiwa was so busy imagining that big boat that he didn't look into his own canoe before he stepped in.

"Ugh!" Saturiwa shouted, as he slipped and fell hard into the canoe. The legs and antennae of hundreds of shrimp were wiggling and tickling all over his skin. He leaped out of the canoe, flinging shrimp in all directions. They were in his hair, stuck to his loincloth! Ugh! And his canoe! It was swamped, and it reeked of shrimp. Saturiwa slapped the clinging shrimp from his arms and legs. His skin stunk! He would never get that smell off before the hunt!

Tenerife paused to let the boys' laughter quiet down.

Emisu held his stomach and rolled on the ground gasping. "He had shrimp in his loincloth? I would love to see Atore like that!"

"Well, that was part of the plan—to make Saturiwa so mad he couldn't think straight. And I did it."

"Yeah, and you made sure he knew it was you because of the shrimp! What was the rest of the plan, Anacotima?"

Tenerife smiled. "I'll tell you."

13

Springing the Trap

I knew Saturiwa would come, so I watched silently between the poles of the weir. The tide had risen so much that I couldn't stand on the bottom anymore. I held onto the weir poles and waited. Just as I had planned, Saturiwa came storming up the creek bank. His face was dark and angry. For a moment, I was scared. He looked like a warrior before battle. Maybe this hadn't been such a good idea.

Then I saw it—a lone shrimp bouncing along, caught in Saturiwa's hair. It looked like it was dancing on his head. I laughed out loud. I couldn't help it. Then I covered my mouth. Had Saturiwa heard me?

I peeked through the south fence. The chief's nephew was charging right through the water—straight at me! That wasn't the plan. He was supposed to walk up the weir from the open end, so I could climb out the back of the trap.

This was not good. I backed up against the far side of the trap. Saturiwa was more than a footstep taller than me. He was never supposed to catch me! I looked around wildly. It was nearly dark. The women should be here by now, to help carry the fish back to the village. Where were they? If Saturiwa caught me out here alone, he could do anything. He could say it was an accident. No one would ever know.

"Did he beat you, Anacotima?"

"Shhh, Kidawe. Let him tell us."

I grabbed at the top of the cane fence, but the weir poles were too tall. I leaped again, splashing down hard and swallowing a mouthful of salt water. In the deepening tide, I couldn't get a good bounce to launch myself over the top. I pressed my face to the cane poles, looking for Saturiwa. Nothing. I looked through another spot and another. Something told me to look up. Saturiwa's hand was reaching over the wall of the weir. His voice sounded dark and dangerous.

"I've got you, Shrimp."

Fig. S. Young Saturiwa and the shrimp

I felt my blood beating in my neck and chest. What had I been thinking? Who cared if Saturiwa led a men's hunt?

The fence in front of me bowed slightly. Saturiwa was climbing over. I had no more time. I lunged sideways and swam for the barrier. That was my only chance. I couldn't hear the women anywhere, so I was on my own. I swam as fast as I could through the salty water. It was hopeless. Saturiwa was ten times faster than me. But what else could I do? I heard a splash as Saturiwa tumbled into the weir behind me.

Then, a woman's voice called out, "Saturiwa, what are you doing?"

It was the chief's second wife. The women were here—finally. I stopped swimming and hung onto the cane fence. Saturiwa had stopped too.

She asked again, "Saturiwa, what about the hunt?"

Saturiwa squinted while he thought. Then he glared over at me. He knew. He was a hunter, and he was standing in a fish trap on the day of the hunt. He was unclean and unfit to join the others.

"Yeah!" I thought. Let's see how he likes being the unclean Shrimpariwa. Maybe that would teach him not to push everyone around.

I swam out of the weir, breathing hard but grinning like a bobcat. Time to collect my shrimp from Saturiwa's canoe. I could hear shouting by the waterside as I worked. The men were refusing to let Saturiwa lead the hunt. He was bad luck now. It would be too risky.

"And you got away with it?" Emisu asked. "Didn't you get in trouble?"

"More trouble than you've been in your entire life."

"But what happened?"

Just then, Emisu's cousin ducked in through the council house doorway. He was leading his little sister, Leena, and about forty other children. Most of them were crying.

"Cousin!" Simaru called out. "Have you been in here with Tenerife all night?"

"Just for a story, because Kidawe was crying," Emisu said.

"Was not!" said Kidawe.

Tenerife cut their argument short. "What's going on, Simaru?" he asked.

"The women sent me to get you, Anacotima. When you weren't in your wife's hut, I started looking for you. These kids were sitting around their fires crying. Most of their dads are on the hunt, and their mothers are helping with Kateema's baby. The women are worried about the storm, Anacotima. They think Huque may be coming. Haven't you heard the winds?"

Tenerife watched the children's eyes widen when they heard the word "Huque." He had lived through many of the great storms. But most of these little ones only remembered darkness and noise and fear in the night. Huque hadn't visited their village for six winters. Perhaps they were due for a visit, but not this night.

"Simaru, come here."

"Yes, Anacotima."

"I want you to give the women a message," Tenerife said. "I cannot enter the birthing hut. It might bring bad luck to Kateema and her baby. You are still young enough to enter. Tell them that these winds are not the call of Huque."

"But how can you know, Anacotima?" Simaru asked. "Palm fronds are ripping away from our roofs. One of the **drying racks** has blown over. The winds are strong. How can you be sure?"

"The **waving crabs** told me, Simaru. During the season of

Huque, I visit the marsh each morning to watch the small crabs. They know the secrets of Huque. A day or two before Huque arrives, the crabs crawl into trees to escape the rising waters. But this morning, the crabs were all near their muddy burrows, sunning and eating and fighting. If Huque was coming, they would move away from the water. And we would do the same. Tell the women that Huque will not come this night. Hurry."

"Thank you, Anacotima." Simaru ran out of the council house to carry the message.

"Where did you learn that?" Kidawe asked. "How did you learn the language of the waving crabs?"

"I learned many things while I lived with the Calusa. Some things I didn't want to know."

A small voice asked, "What did you learn, Anacotima?"

Tenerife turned to see who had spoken. It was Leena, Simaru's little sister. She stared back at him with wide wet eyes.

Tenerife smiled gently. "Come and sit down. I'll tell you the story."

Timucua People

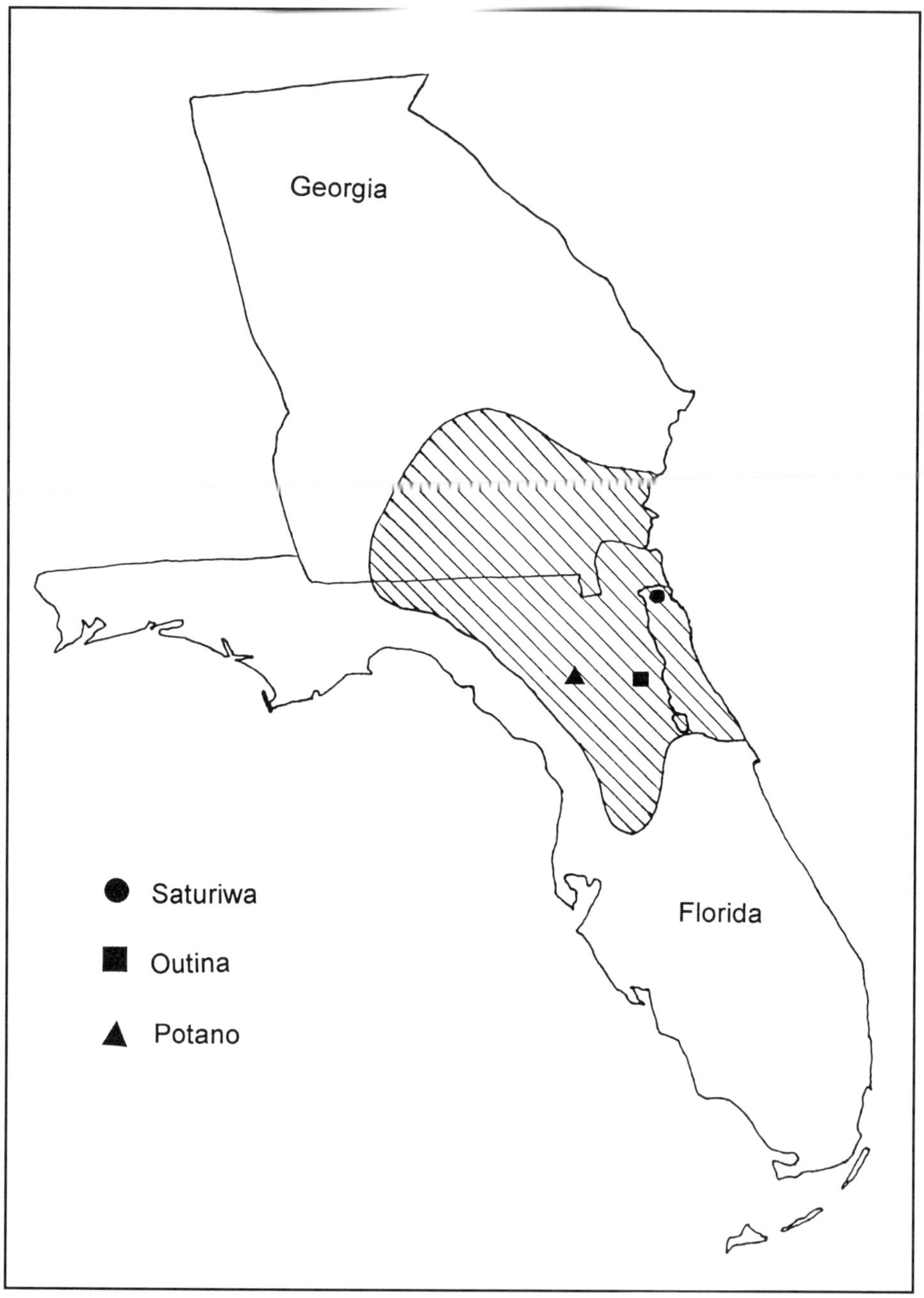

Fig. T. Map of Timucua territory

14

A Big Misunderstanding

Now you know the basics about Florida's early people. But you still don't know the whole story. Each native group had its own special way of life. Tenerife, Kidawe, Emisu, and Saturiwa were Timucua people, so let's find out more about the Timucua (Ti-MOO-kwa).

The Timucua Indians lived in north and central Florida and in southeast Georgia. (See Figure T.) Although they spoke the same language, they were never united into one tribe. In fact, some Timucua villages fought against each other. Speaking the same language meant these villages could trade easily, share ideas and inventions, and argue over resources. Who gets to use the best fishing spot? Who gets to hunt the herd of deer that keeps crossing the river? Sometimes villages that were friends in winter would be enemies by summer.

When the French and Spanish got to Florida, they didn't realize the Timucua people were made up of several different groups. They thought: same language, same tribe. So they called them all by the same name. But where did that name come from?

French explorers may have had something to do with it. When they visited Florida in 1562, they met a chief who had some silver pieces. They asked him, "Where did you get that silver?" Chief Saturiwa couldn't speak French, but he could tell that the strangers were interested in his silver. So he pointed across the river and said, "I captured it from Thimogona." The French remembered the word "Thimagona" and started calling all of the nearby native people Thimogona or Timagoa or Timogua or Timucua. That may be how the name got started. (The native people probably never called themselves by this name.)

Historians think the word "Thimagona" meant "enemy." Chief Saturiwa may have been talking about Chief Outina, his greatest enemy. But where did Chief Outina get the silver? He couldn't have dug it up in Florida.

At that time, Spanish soldiers were forcing the Indians in Mexico to dig up silver and load it onto ships. These treasure ships sailed south around Florida, then northeast across the

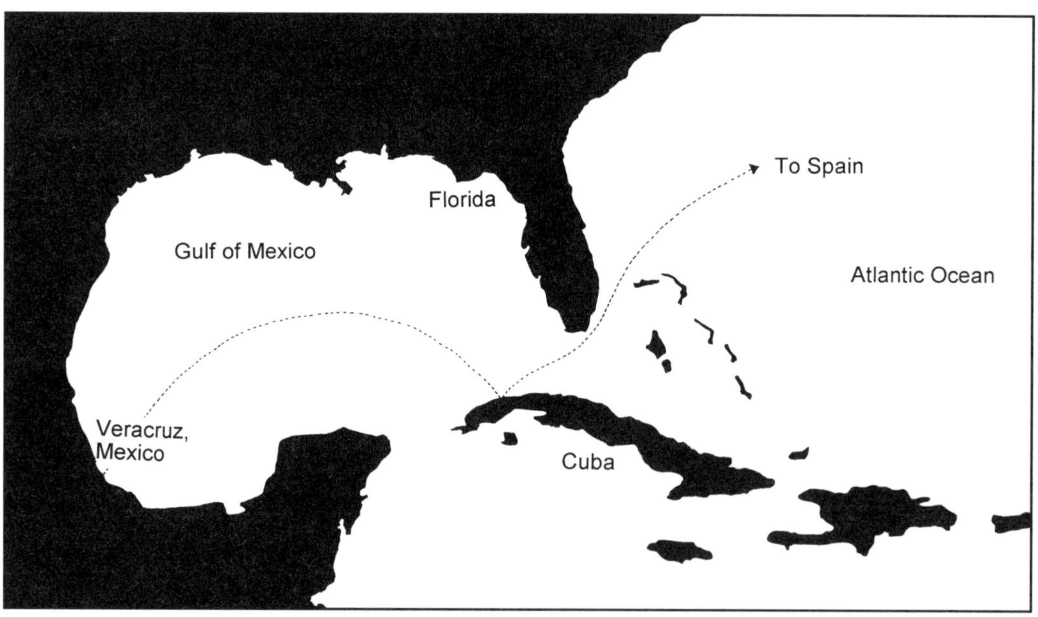

Fig. U. Map showing how silver traveled from Mexico to Spain

Atlantic Ocean toward Spain. (See Figure U.) Sometimes, the ships ran into storms before they made it around Florida. If they sank, some of their cargo washed up on Florida's beaches. Native people could pick up anything they wanted. Outina's silver probably came from a shipwreck on Florida's western beaches. But the Europeans thought this silver came from Florida, and they spent a lot of time and energy searching for more. You'll learn more about the Europeans in chapter 39.

15

Chiefs and Beliefs

Saturiwa and Outina were headchiefs who ruled more than 30 villages. Saturiwa's villages, located on the east side of the St. Johns River, did not get along with Outina's villages to the west. Chief Potano's main village was even farther west, near where Gainesville is today. He sometimes fought wars with Outina. Chief Cubaconi ruled several Timucua villages in Georgia. Although most chiefs were men, some, like Cubaconi, were women.

Because Timucua villages were located across such a large area, the people adapted to many different environments. In central Florida and south Georgia the soil was very rich. The Timucua living in these areas could plant and harvest a good crop every year. They still went fishing, hunting, and gathering, but corn was an important part of their diet.

In east Florida, sandy soils made it difficult to grow crops. The Timucua living there spent more time and energy on plant gathering, fishing, and hunting than on gardening.

Wherever the Timucua lived, they had similar ideas about chiefs, clans, and tattoos. Chiefs were always members of the White Deer Clan. There were many other clans, including Panther, Earth, and Fish. Girls and boys were automatically in their mother's clan. If you were Timucua, your clan would include your brothers and sisters, your mother, and most of her relatives. Your father and his relatives would *not* be in your clan.

Timucua people couldn't marry anyone in their own clan. That would be like marrying a cousin. Since a chief could not marry anyone in his clan, his children wouldn't be in the White Deer Clan. They could never be chiefs. The chief's sister was in the White Deer Clan, so her children could become chiefs. This usually meant that a chief's oldest nephew would become the next chief. Uncles trained nephews while they were growing up, and mothers trained daughters. That way, children were always taught by someone in their own clan.

While only people in the White Deer Clan could rule a village, other people played important roles. The shaman was in charge of religion and medicine. Some shamans, called *isucu*, studied medicine plants and worked as healers. Other shamans, called *jarva*, helped the chief understand the spirit world. The *jarva* could be asked to foretell the future, bring good luck to a hunt, or put a curse on someone. The chief also had noble advisors called *anacotimas*. These men advised the chief on hunting, weather, trading, and battle. Female chiefs, like Cubaconi, had women as advisors.

Both male and female chiefs were heavily tattooed to show their status, strength, and bravery. They put permanent dotted designs on their skin with a bone needle and ashes. The ashes added color and helped to stop infections. Any Timucua person could earn tattoos, and the more tattoos a person had, the more important he or she was in the village. The chief and his noble advisors had more tattoos than anyone else. (Look ahead at figure YY on page 198.)

16

Hunting on the Land

The Timucua were skilled with many hunting and fishing tools. (See figure V.) These tools helped them find food in grassy marshes and in forests thick with trees, shrubs, and tangling vines.

Fire was a useful hunting tool for the Timucua people. They set carefully planned fires that forced prey animals to run right toward waiting Timucua hunters. These fires also burned up some of the shrubs and vines, making it easier for hunters to see animals hiding in the forest. With some of the trees burned out, more sunshine reached the ground, helping grasses and wild-flowers to grow. The Timucua could gather these edible plants or leave them to attract prey animals like tortoises and deer. Fire was a dangerous but effective Timucua tool. (Today, setting fires is illegal unless you are a trained forester.)

The Timucua hunted deer with another special tool called a deer cloak—a whole deerskin with the legs and antlers still attached. Hunters covered themselves with a deer cloak and crouched down on all fours, so they looked like deer. That way, they could creep up close to a herd without scaring the deer away. Then they could shoot the deer with their bows and arrows. (See figure W.)

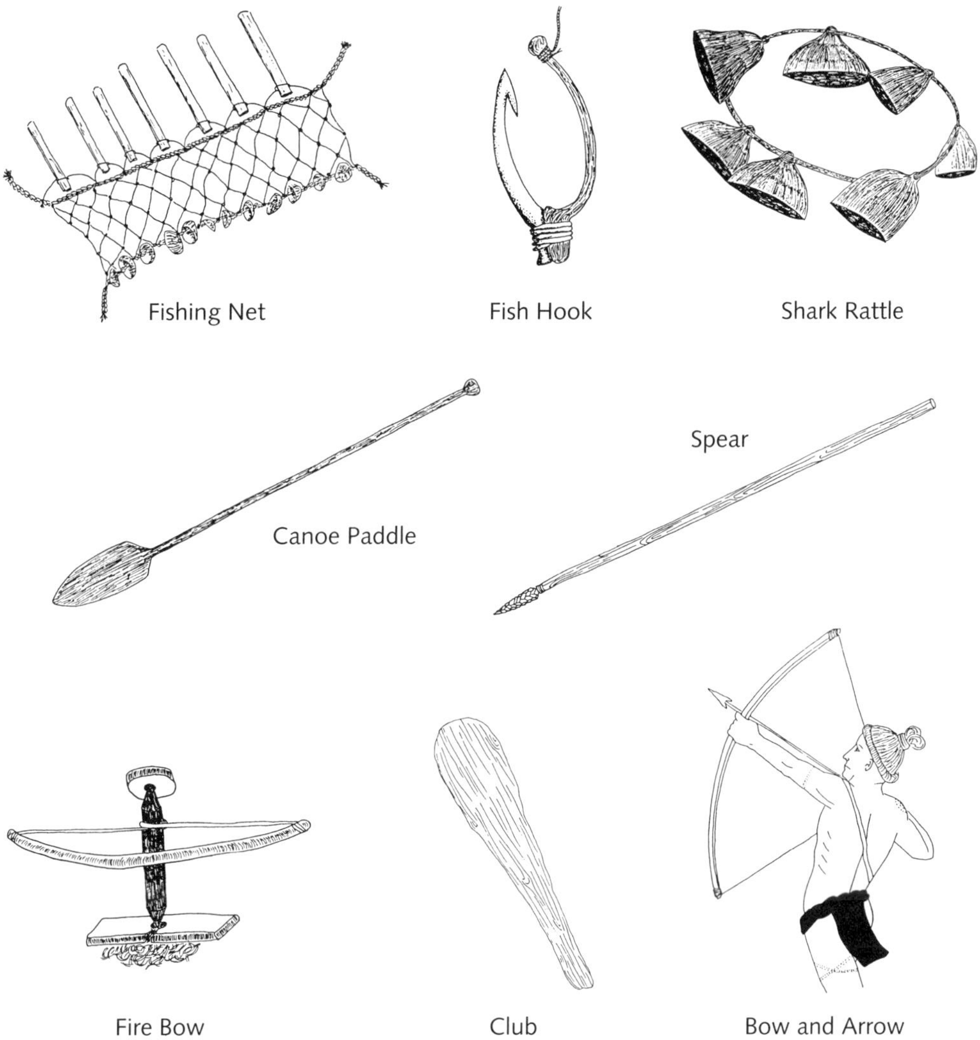

Fig. V. Native hunting and fishing tools

The Timucua also hunted alligators. There are stories of 20-foot gators in early Florida, but even a 12-foot alligator can be deadly. When hunting them, the Timucua stuck one end of a long pole in the alligator's mouth. They used this pole to flip the alligator over, exposing its softer belly. Then they used spears, clubs, and bows and arrows to finish the hunt. (See figure X.)

Fig. W. French engraving of a deer hunt, by Theodore de Bry

Fig. X. French engraving of an alligator hunt, by Theodore de Bry

17

Drawings and Stories

Many French and Spanish people, including Jacques le Moyne, Theodore de Bry, and Francisco Pareja, drew pictures and wrote stories about the Timucua. In 1564, Jacques le Moyne, a French mapmaker, painted many pictures of the Timucua. Later, Theodore de Bry used these paintings to engrave pictures for a book. You've already seen some of de Bry's **engravings**, and you'll see more in the coming chapters. They tell us a lot about the Timucua. The deer-hunt engraving shows examples of Timucua deer cloaks, while the alligator hunt teaches us how they used poles to hunt these large reptiles. But there are some *big* mistakes in de Bry's engravings. Look back at the deer hunt and alligator hunt in figures W and X on page 76.

(1) Do the antlers on Florida deer look like that?

(2) Could anyone get that close to a wild deer?

(3) Can you see reflections in north Florida rivers?

(4) Were alligators 80 feet long back then?

(5) Do alligators have eyebrows?

(6) Would the Timucua hunt two gators at once?

(7) Would they hunt without wearing protective clothing?

The answer to each of these questions is no. How did these errors get into the engravings? Historians think that the original artist, le Moyne, drew the details correctly. They believe de Bry made the changes when he engraved them. When studying old drawings, historians always try to figure out which parts are true and which parts are not.

Another way historians learn about the Timucua Indians is by reading a book called the *Confessionario.* This book was written by Francisco Pareja, a Spanish priest who lived in Florida. He wanted to help other priests teach the Timucua about Christianity. However, most of these Spanish priests did not speak the Timucua language. To help them, Pareja translated the Spanish words each priest should say into the Timucua language. Modern historians can use this book to learn how the Timucua spoke and study what they believed.

When we study the *Confessionario*, we have to remember two important things. First, while Pareja tried to write the Timucua sentences correctly, he may have made mistakes. Also, he only used about 1,400 Timucua words. There were many more words in the Timucua language, but we may never find out what they were. Second, Pareja tried to understand Timucua beliefs, but he probably made mistakes. Since he was Spanish, the things he wrote tell us more about what the Spanish were thinking, than what the Timucua were thinking.

Here is an example from Pareja's book, a question Spanish priests asked Timucua people during confession.

In English: "The first fish that enters the new fish traps, have you said not to put them in hot water, otherwise no more will be caught?"

In Spanish: *"El primer pescado, que entra en la pesquera nueva, has dicho no lo echen en agua caliente, que no se cojera mas?"*

In Timucua: *"Ychali ele iribosobinaco, cuyuma, ubuata, quibenco melasonolehabetile, cuyuma, naqua ubuahauetile, naquosatiquanima camobicho?"*

We can study at least two things in this example: the ideas and the words. Pareja was asking the Timucua about an idea. Did they believe it would bring bad luck if they cooked the first fish they caught in a new trap? When the Timucua said yes, the priest told them they were wrong, because this belief did not match Christian beliefs.

Even today, people might wonder about this idea. How could throwing the first fish back help them catch more fish later? A Timucua person might explain it this way. "If people hunted every fish from the river, there wouldn't be any left to catch. The people would starve. But, if we always throw back the first fish from a new trap, there will always be a few fish out there to have more babies." When you think it through, it makes sense.

Now, let's look at the Timucua language. The words seem long because the Timucua hooked several words together that we separate in English. Instead of saying "the fish" the way English speakers do, Timucua speakers said "fish-the." "The" goes at the end of the word. In Timucua, "fish" is "*cuyu.*" "The" is "*-ma.*" So, "the fish" is "*cuyu-ma.*" Can you find the word "*cuyuma*" in the Timucua sentence?

Here are a few examples of how the Timucua language works. Try saying these words aloud to get a feel for how this language sounded.

English		*Timucua*	*English phrases*		*Timucua phrases*
the	=	*-ma*	the deer	=	*honoso-ma*
her	=	*-si*	her deer	=	*honoso-si*
I am	=	*hontala*	the son	=	*chiri-ma*
son	=	*chiri*	her son	=	*chiri-si*
deer	=	*honoso*	I am strong.	=	*Hontala tari.*
strong	=	*tari*	I am her son.	=	*Hontala chiri-si.*

18

Fighting for Ashefa

New characters in this section:

Belesi (Be-LEH-see): A six-year-old Timucua boy
Nede (NEH-deh): A seven-year-old Timucua boy
Sheko (Sheh-ko): A forty-five-year-old escaped African slave
Teceta (Te-SE-ta): A five-year-old Timucua boy

Tenerife flinched at a sudden crack of thunder. The children's small bodies pressed close to him, their sniffling sobs blending with the sounds of the storm. Lightning brightened the smoke hole, and Tenerife looked closely at the forty children around him. They ranged in age from two to eleven winters. The smallest ones gripped soft rabbit-skin blankets with tiny fingers.

"Children," Tenerife said, "we must get ready for a tale. If you are more than five winters old, I want you to find a younger child to sit with. If they are small enough, let them sit in your lap."

Emisu grinned and elbowed Kidawe. "Come on, my nephew." Emisu laughed. "Come to Uncle!"

Kidawe made a face at him and shrugged away. He walked over to Tenerife. "Why didn't you say more than *four* winters, so I could be one of the big kids too?"

While the children giggled and argued, Tenerife dragged a

large clay bowl to the edge of the hearth fire. He hefted a leather water bag to his shoulder and carefully filled the bowl. Then he sat back slowly against his leaning bench. The fire would heat the tea water during his tale. Both he and the children would need to wet their throats on this stormy night. Finally, all of the children were settled, poking and teasing and giggling. Tenerife could barely hear the soothing chant from the women's hut where Kateema's baby would be born. He took a deep breath and began.

"We have hunted a mammoth and trapped the nephew of a chief," he said. "But the journey I took at eleven winters old is even more exciting."

"Where did you travel to?" Emisu asked.

"I almost traveled to the spirit world." Tenerife turned an ear to the storm. The winds had begun to howl in the oddest way. He had heard that sound before, but he couldn't remember when. Better to start his tale before the children noticed it too.

My trap for Saturiwa had worked. The men refused to let him lead the seal hunt. I bragged to everyone that I had finally made him pay. But I didn't know the whole story.

"What do you mean?" little Leena asked.

The chief had been planning a manhood ceremony for Saturiwa. But until his nephew led a group hunt, there could be no ceremony. The next big hunt wouldn't be until the winter moon. Saturiwa would have to wait a long time to become a man.

"What happened?" Simaru asked.

They let Saturiwa decide my punishment. And since he couldn't lead a hunt until the winter moon, I was forbidden to touch a hunting weapon until that time.

"They wouldn't let you hunt?" Emisu said. "But you were eleven winters old, like me! Weren't you practicing for your first adult hunt?"

"I had been, but that all ended the moment I tricked Saturiwa into the weir. I was forbidden to use a hunting weapon of any kind. I wasn't even allowed to practice at the target field."

"But that's not fair!" Emisu shouted.

"Maybe it wasn't fair, but the chief had his own worries. The villages to the west of the river were causing trouble, stealing corn from our fields and hunting deer on our side of the river. The chief needed Saturiwa to lead men in battle—for the good of all the people. My stunt had put the whole village in danger.

"What did you do?" Emisu asked.

I didn't hunt. I practiced tracking animals when I could, but the women kept me busy—grinding corn, scaling fish, mending nets, watching babies—anything they could think of. I carried water from the spring and scraped animal hides. I coiled pottery and dried meat. They even made me pound moss cloth for the girls' new outfits.

The boys in the crowd squirmed as Tenerife spoke. They didn't like the idea of doing women's work.

I did it though. I did every single chore, even when Saturiwa called me a girl-child. And I never hunted, either.

"Until?" Simaru asked. "You never hunted until?"

Tenerife nodded. The wind was momentarily quiet. All of the children's eyes were dry and waiting.

You're right, Simaru. I finally did hunt. But I never used a hunting weapon; I never broke the rule. After the chief announced my pun-

ishment, none of the kids would talk to me, not even Ashefa. Their parents wouldn't let them. It was a lonely time.

One afternoon, I was hauling wet clay to the women's workspace, hoping to visit with Ashefa. But Saturiwa was already there. He was handing her a present—a beautiful comb, carved from a white whelk shell.

"But why did he give her a present?" Simaru asked.

She was a beautiful girl, Tenerife said, smiling at the memory. I didn't know if Saturiwa really liked her, or if he was just trying to make me angry. But I couldn't believe my eyes when Ashefa accepted his gift.

"Didn't she know you wanted to marry her?" Emisu asked. "Hadn't you told her?"

Fig. Y. Young Ashefa coiling pottery

Tenerife grinned. I never even thought about it, Emisu. We had always been together. We would always be together. Who thinks about marriage at eleven winters old? When I saw Ashefa accept that comb, I started thinking about it—a lot. I didn't want her to marry anybody else, especially not him.

Every day Saturiwa brought her something he had hunted—beautiful feathers or soft rabbit skins or tendon threads for sewing. And I had nothing to give her. Without hunting, what could I bring her? I followed Saturiwa and Ashefa when I could, listening to them. One day, Saturiwa promised he would hunt her a deer fur to keep her warm during the winter moon. That would prove he would make a good husband.

"Husband!" Simaru shouted. "He did want to marry her!"

"At least that's what he told her. If she agreed, she would have to marry him when she got to be 15 winters. I almost rushed out and—"

"And what?" Kidawe asked.

"I didn't know what to do!" Tenerife said. "I had to prove I would be a good husband. I had to get Ashefa a deer fur—before Saturiwa did."

"But you couldn't touch a weapon!" Emisu said.

"I know, and I never did. But I did come up with a plan."

19

Deer Hunt

The tea water popped and boiled, and Tenerife tossed in a handful of dried mint leaves. The wind howled, then quieted. Tenerife looked up at the smoke hole. Everything seemed normal enough, but that sound . . . He shook his head. He would remember sooner or later.

Kidawe tugged on his arm. "What was your plan?"

It took me a few days to get ready, Kidawe. There was a place far to the south that my uncle had showed me. During the blueberry moon, many deer go there to fatten themselves. It was a long journey—a whole day running, but Ashefa was worth it.

"Anacotima," Kidawe interrupted, "how could you hunt without a weapon?"

I remembered the mammoth hunt. Instead of stampeding the deer toward a deep marsh, I would run them toward a pit trap. I packed my chert knife, a fire bow, and a whelk shovel, then filled my water bladder at the spring. I grabbed some deer jerky and took a sharpened digging stick as well, in case I ran into a panther or some wolves. Finally, I packed my deer cloak. It was a training cloak—an old ratty fur from a doe. Many boys had used that cloak to learn their hunting skills. I rolled it tightly and pushed it into my pack.

"And your parents just let you go?" Emisu asked. "My mother would never let me go on a journey like that."

"That's because she knows what could happen," Tenerife said. "I told you I was a foolish boy. I never told my parents that I was leaving."

I planned to be back in five days. One day running, one day digging the pit trap, one day hunting, one day tanning the fur, and another day running home. With any luck, Saturiwa wouldn't have his deer fur ready for Ashefa before then.

I got up before Father Sun rose the next morning, chanted him a greeting, and headed south. Back then I had no limp. I ran like a deer. It was nearly dark when I approached the deer spot.

A woman's voice cried out in the night. Tenerife and the children turned their heads toward the women's hut. They couldn't hear Kateema anymore, only the women's steady chanting. The birth was beginning. Tenerife said a silent good-luck chant for Kateema and her baby. All the signs said the child would be a boy, a great hunter like his grandfather Sheko. Tenerife thought of the dark-skinned man, the friend of his boyhood journeys. Sheko was away on the hunt with the other men, perhaps thinking of his daughter Kateema at this very moment.

"What happened next?" Little Leena tapped him lightly on the arm. "Anacotima, what happened next?"

Tenerife cleared his throat and smiled at the small girl.

When I got there, I tried on the deer cloak. Its head fit right over mine. Its back hid my body, and when I crouched down, its legs hung to the ground—just like a living deer. Even though the deer fur was old and ragged, it made me look just like a small doe. I finished the disguise by smearing some deer droppings on my skin to cover my scent. Finally,

I sat down to rest. I chewed some tough deer jerky and huddled under a blanket of dry leaves to sleep.

"Why didn't you make a fire?" Leena asked.

I couldn't light a fire, because the smoky smell would scare the deer away. The leaves kept me warm enough. Father Sun woke me early the next morning. My knees ached from the last day's run, but Ashefa was worth it. I stumbled behind the tree to pass my water then stopped suddenly.

What was I thinking? The deer would smell that from miles away. I had almost ruined everything! Quietly, I walked out into the edge of the river and passed my water into the slow-flowing current. The river would carry my scent away. Now all I had to do was wait.

I climbed an old oak and settled into the V where the branches started. In time, the deer began to come, mothers with older fawns that were losing their spots, old tired grandfathers with ten points on their antlers, and every kind in between. I saw fourteen deer in the herd. They nibbled on blueberries and swallowed cool water from the river. One doe walked right by the tree I sat in. If only I could've used my bow!

The fawns leaped about, butting the adult males in play, then dashing away. I didn't want to disturb their peace, but I had come to hunt. I would thank my prey for its sacrifice and honor it all my days. I was eager for night to come.

When the sky began to darken, the deer moved away. I unfolded my cramped knees and climbed down out of the tree. I planned to dig my pit trap on a high patch of ground, not far from the river. I needed to dig down at least two footsteps. With luck, I'd dig that deep before any water seeped in from underground. Digging mud was harder than digging dry dirt. Two footsteps would be deep enough to slow a running deer. Then I could club it with my shell shovel. The deer would die quickly, with little pain, and I would sing songs of its death all during my journey home.

Tenerife paused to listen. For the first time that night, rain fell fast and strong, pelting the roof of the hut. Spatters blew in through the high smoke hole. Tenerife gripped his feather matchcoat tighter around him and turned an ear to the moaning wind.

"Ow!" Emisu jumped up, rubbing his shoulder. He picked up the chunk of ice that had hit him.

"It's hailing," Tenerife said. "Let's get away from the smoke hole. We'll move the fire over there." The children just looked at each other. The hearth fire always stayed in the same place. "Now, children," Tenerife commanded. "Let's go."

Emisu flexed his shoulder and stood up. "You heard Anacotima," he said. "Over there, by the guest area." The children started moving, but not very fast. They shoved and giggled and argued. Tenerife listened more closely to the howl of the wind, trying to hear over the children's noise. Suddenly, he remembered when he'd heard that sound before.

"Move!" he shouted. All the children stared at him. They had never heard Tenerife raise his voice. "Move now! Run!"

They ran. Tenerife was barely out from under the smoke hole when water crashed through it. Rain and chunks of icy hail poured down, tearing palm fronds and center supports from the roof. The downpour drenched the fire pit and the ground around it. The fire went out.

It was totally dark.

20

Capture

For a moment, everything was silent. The women's chanting had stopped, and the rain had ceased as well. Tenerife listened. It was not Huque. But tornadoes could come in a storm like this. He looked up to check the damage to the roof but could see nothing in the blackness.

Then he heard the first sniffle. "I want Mommy," Leena whispered. Her tiny fingers had found Tenerife's thumb and gripped his rough skin tightly. Other sobs and tears joined hers. Tenerife closed his eyes. If only Ashefa were here. She was so much better with the youngest children. Tenerife listened again for the women's chanting.

No sound emerged from the women's hut. He stood up as straight as his bad leg would hold him. "My children, we have two jobs. First, Emisu and Simaru must run to the women's hut to check on their safety. We are the only men in the village right now, and we must protect our women."

The older boys stood. "We'll go," they said.

"Watch the storm," Tenerife whispered.

With quiet stealth, the boys crept through the dark hut. Neither tripped or made a sound as they left. Tenerife spoke to the younger children. "Now, we've got to get a fire going."

"How?" Kidawe's voice trembled, but he didn't cry.

"Well, Kidawe, if you can get a fire bow from the guest area and choose three helpers, I would like you lead the fire team." Tenerife listened as Kidawe bumped into and stumbled over child after child.

Their voices jumbled together as Kidawe passed. "Watch it, Kidawe!" "Ow, that's my hand." "Look where you're stepping!"

Finally, the children stopped complaining and started to giggle. "Wait, Kidawe, you missed my hand!" "Can't you step on me too?"

"Very funny," Kidawe said, fumbling around in the darkness. "Hey, I found it!"

Kidawe chose his team to help him carry the fire-making tools—the fire bow, fire stick, and **fire board**, plus the tinder and fuel.

Kidawe and his team stumbled back through the darkness and set down their tools. Tenerife laid the fire board flat on the ground and held it in place with one foot on each end. He patted around to find the small hole in the board. Then he stuffed a little cattail fluff tinder underneath to catch sparks. Tenerife set the fire stick upright in the fire board's hole as he listened to Kidawe arranging the corncobs and wood chips. Finally, he said "here, Kidawe." In the dark, Tenerife helped Kidawe loop the fire bow tightly around the stick. "You're in charge, Kidawe. Make us a fire." He whispered a silent good-luck chant for the boys. Starting a fire with a fire bow took concentration and strength. It would be hard to do in total darkness.

Kidawe took charge of the fire team. "I'll go first, then you Teceta, then Belesi, then Nede. Are you ready, men?"

Tenerife smiled at the boys calling themselves men. They were only five, six, and seven winters. But why not? They were acting like adults. "Yes, men," Tenerife said. "Are you ready?"

"We are, Anacotima," Kidawe answered.

Tenerife strained his eyes to see Kidawe, but it was too dark. He pictured the boy working the fire bow, pushing the bow away from him and pulling it back again. Away and back, away and back. Each time he worked the bow, the fire stick would spin against the fire board. Back and forth, back and forth. After a while, Kidawe tired, and Tenerife heard Teceta take his place. By the time it was Belesi's turn, the other children were chanting, giving the boys a rhythm to work to. "Fire, fi-re, fi-re." When Nede took over, he had only worked the bow a few times when a spark flew off the fire stick. Tenerife tried to scoop it onto the cattail fluff, but it went out.

"Keep going, Nede. We're almost there." Tenerife tilted the fire board with his feet to angle it toward the fluff. Nede worked the bow, back and forth, back and forth. Then another spark jumped right onto the fluff. Tenerife carefully blew on it, giving the fire air to breathe. The spark grew into a tiny flame. Tenerife scooped up the burning fluff and gently set it onto the corncobs. He blew on it again, and soon the flames were bright enough to light all the children's faces. "Good job, men," Tenerife said.

The other children slapped the fire makers on the back, laughing. "Yeah, good job, men!"

Emisu and Simaru ducked back in through the bearskin door cover. A gust of wind entered with them, licking at the new fire, making it burn bright and hot. "Look," they said, holding a burning stick, "we brought a torch!"

"We don't need it," Kidawe answered. "The men here took care of it."

Emisu and Simaru looked at each other and shrugged.

"How's Kateema?" Kidawe asked. "And Mother?"

"They're all fine," Emisu said. "Their fire went out too. That's why the chanting stopped. We brought them a torch from the next hut and got their fire going again."

"Tenerife," Simaru said, "how did you know the rain would pour in?"

"It's called a **sky spill**. I have only seen it happen once before. But the sound it makes, do you remember how the wind howled? That's the cry of a sky spill. Nothing else makes a sound like that."

"Will it happen again, Anacotima?" Emisu asked.

"No one can know," said Tenerife. Everyone looked up at the large ragged hole in the roof. The wind still whipped through the council house, pulling at torn palm fronds, but it was just a normal wind.

"What happened on your deer hunt?" Emisu asked, calling the children's attention away from the storm.

Tenerife smiled his approval. "Let's get a new pot of tea going first, to wet this storyteller's throat." Several boys filled a pot with water as Tenerife began.

It was a long night. Digging that pit took every bit of my strength and patience. The ground was thick with tree roots that slowed my digging. I hit the ground with my digging tool, then scooped up the loose soil and spread it around the hole. The pit was six footsteps long, but I had dug only one footstep deep when water started seeping in. Digging through the heavy mud took ten times as long.

Father Sun was sending pink streaks through the morning sky when I stopped digging. My back and shoulders ached from the work, and the pit was barely two footsteps deep. The more I dug, the more it caved in and filled up with mud. I slogged out of the hole and cut ten small maple trees. I laid the trees criss-cross over the pit and tossed maple leaves and palmetto fronds over them to camouflage the trap.

Morning had come bright and clear—a good day for a hunt. I breathed in the warm morning air and whispered a good-luck chant. Next, I gathered more deer ***scat*** *and smeared it into the mud that already coated me from head to toe. Finally I picked up my tools, put on my deer cloak, and crouched in the blueberry bushes to wait.*

I chanted a greeting to Father Sun and chewed a piece of venison. I didn't want my stomach to growl and scare the deer away. One by one, the deer returned. First the mothers and nearly grown fawns. I let them pass the trap and made no noise. One fawn looked right at me. Inside the deer cloak, I turned my head to make it look like I was nibbling a blueberry. The fawn flicked its tail and moved off.

I whispered a silent thank you to Father Sun for the good luck. Time passed, but finally, the older male deer came to drink. I was about to leap out shouting—to stampede them toward my pit trap—when I heard a strange noise. It sounded like a—

Lightning brightened the smoke hole, and everyone looked up, waiting for the thunder. When the rumbling stopped, Kidawe leaned forward and asked "What did you hear, Anacotima? Was it the sky spill?"

No, Kidawe, it wasn't a sky spill. It was a click. Not a wind sound, or a bug sound, or a bird sound, or a deer sound. Then I heard it again. I couldn't see much from inside the bushes, so I listened quietly.

A thunderclap slapped the air. One of the deer staggered sideways and fell. Then thunder clapped again, and another deer dropped. What was happening? The herd stampeded south along the river, leaping and bounding away from the horrible sounds. A young buck stumbled into my trap, his thin legs sinking in the muddy pit. I wanted to leap out and hunt him, but my eyes were glued to the other two deer. What was killing them?

One deer lay still, but the other one kicked wildly and screamed a horrible deer song. What had done this? No hunter of the people would let a deer die in agony like that. Its death would have been swift and merciful. I watched the animal twist and kick, until finally, its struggle ended. Then I looked back at my small buck. He had nearly escaped the muddy pit trap. His thin toes grasped at the branches I had used to cover the trap. From my hiding spot, I looked around for the strange spirit that had killed the deer, but I couldn't see anything.

Then I heard footsteps behind me. I stayed perfectly still and quiet, like a fawn away from its mother. I could see the buck's eyes widen with terror. He could see what was killing his people, but I could not.

Bang! Another thunderclap broke the silence.

I yelped.

I couldn't help it. I was so surprised. I barely had time to see the buck fall before thunder clapped again.

"What happened, Anacotima?"

Fig. Z. Deer caught in Tenerife's pit trap

I didn't know, Simaru. I thought the spirit who had killed the deer was killing me too. Pain shot through my right hip and up into my back. The spirit beasts started into the bushes after me, so I dragged myself away from them. My right leg wouldn't work, but I crawled anyway. The spirit beasts shouted strange words at me, but I didn't stop. One of them picked me up and stripped off my deer cloak.

I tried to fight this spirit beast, pulling at his hairy face and strange clothes, but I was too weak. He tied my hands and legs and threw me over his shoulder. The other spirit beasts gathered up the deer and gutted them there, wasting the ***entrails****, and dishonoring the spirit of the animals. Then they started walking, with me tied and slung just like a slaughtered deer.*

"What happened next, Anacotima?"

I tried to pay attention to our path so I could escape later. But I couldn't. I felt blood oozing down my leg. It dripped slowly from my hip down to my big toe as the spirit beasts stomped through the forest. I didn't realize how badly I'd been hurt. My own spirit fled, and I lost consciousness.

"Is that how you got your limp, Anacotima?" Emisu jumped up and walked toward Tenerife. "When you were only eleven winters?"

Tenerife nodded and stood to let them see the jagged dent left by the bullet's track.

He reached over to the pot of tea water and dipped a finger in to see if it was hot enough. Small faces watched him intently, ignoring the thunder that clapped sharply outside. "Let's have some tea, children. Then we'll have another story."

Calusa People

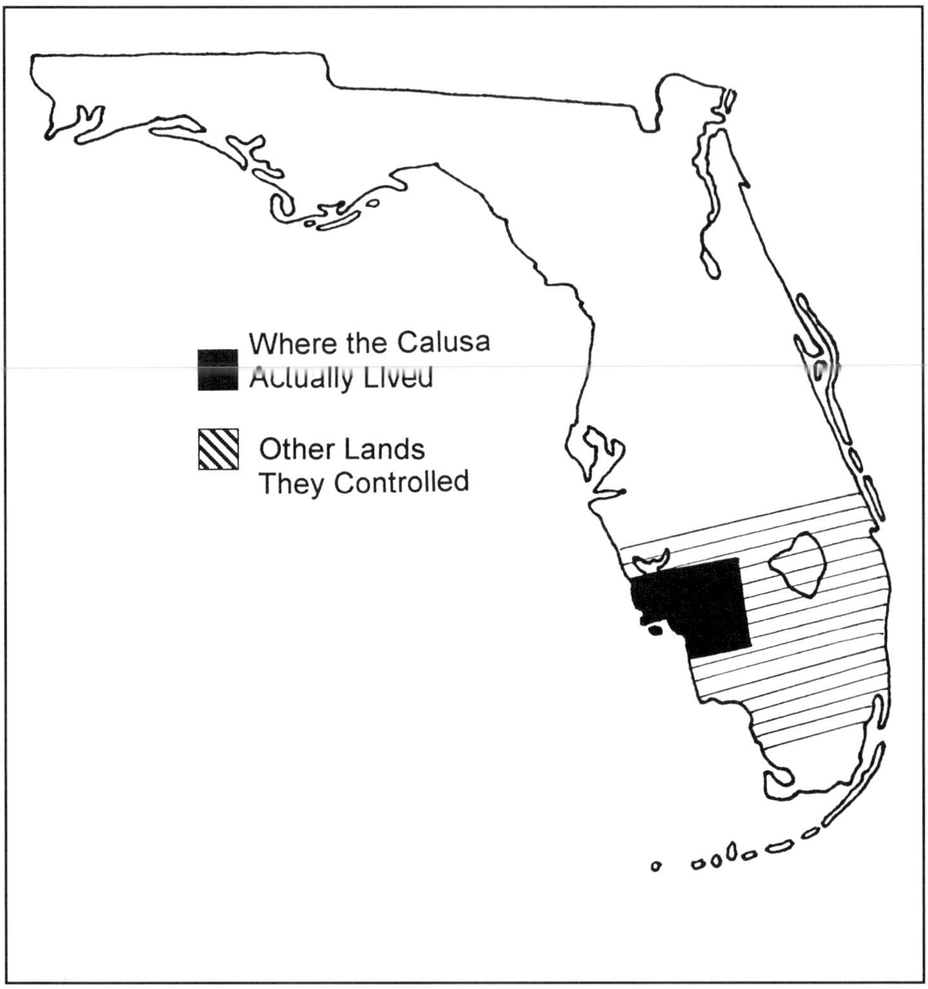

Fig. AA. Map of Calusa territory

21

Calusa Power

The name "Calusa" (Kuh-LOO-suh) probably meant "fierce people." In the 1500s, the Calusa controlled most of southwest Florida. At times, they ruled the Matecumbe people of the Florida Keys, the Tequesta of the Miami area, and the Tocobago of Tampa Bay. (See figure AA.) These native groups paid tribute in food and supplies, as well as respect, to the Calusa chief.

The center of the Calusa **chiefdom** was Mound Key, an island near the modern city of Ft. Myers. This island was surrounded by rich mangrove swamps, flowing grassy waters, and thick forests. The Calusa people could gather food along nearby rivers or hunt and fish in the open waters of the Gulf of Mexico. This variety of rich habitats helped the Calusa grow powerful.

While the Calusa did gather plant foods and hunt land animals, 90 percent of their food came from the whelks, fish, and sharks they hunted in shallow brackish marshes. (See figure BB.) Most chiefdoms depended on large fields of corn and beans to feed their people, but the Calusa didn't need to grow these crops. They planted only small family gardens of papaya, squash, and peppers. Seafood gave them everything else they needed to raise strong, healthy children.

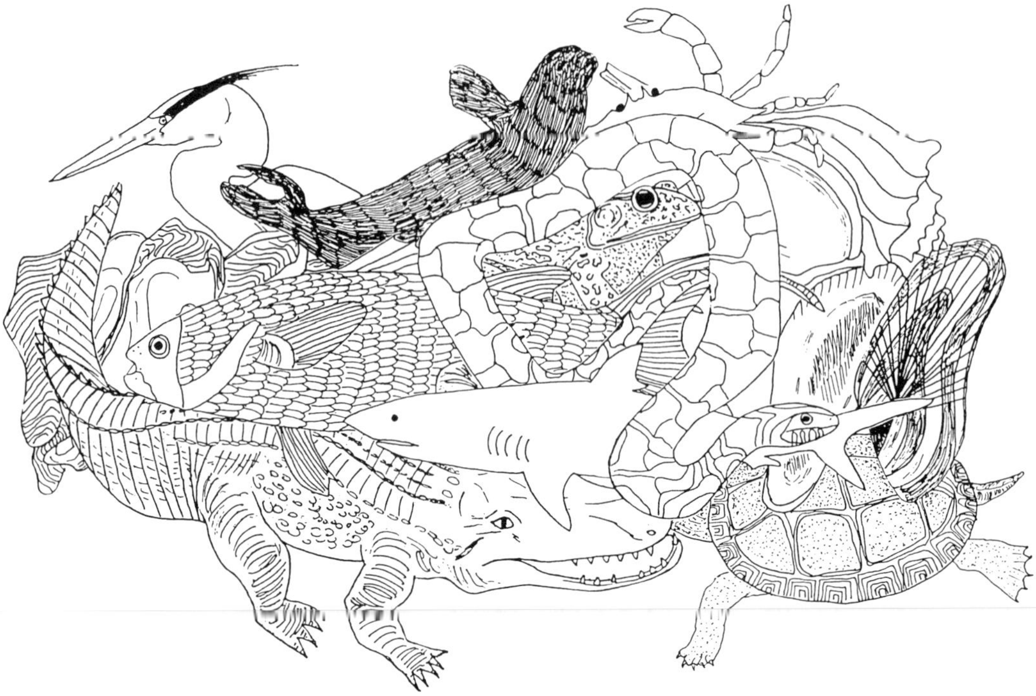

The Calusa ate many water animals, including alligator, crab, fish, frog, heron, mussel, oyster, seal, shark, turtle, and whelk. Can you find these animals in the collage above?

Fig. BB. Water animals native people hunted

These well-fed children grew up and moved to nearby islands or rivers to start their own villages. Soon, there were Calusa villages all over southwest Florida. As their population grew, the Calusa may not have been able to find enough food for everyone. They conquered nearby villages to take some of their food. Because there were so many Calusa people, their leaders could raise armies to force other villages to join the Calusa family.

When Spanish treasure ships wrecked on the coast, the Calusa searched through the ruins. They found silver, metal tools, and even Spanish sailors to keep as slaves. Native groups that lived far from the coast wanted these things too. The Calusa chief rewarded loyal villages and encouraged new ones to join the Calusa chiefdom by sending them gifts of silver, tools, and slaves.

After meeting the Spanish soldiers and priests, the Calusa chief may have felt threatened by their guns and strange ideas. Conquering more villages meant he could call up more warriors to defend his people. With an excellent food source, an army of warriors, and a good location, the Calusa became known as the Fierce People all across Florida.

22

Native Religions

We have learned about the Calusa religion from a Spanish priest named Father Rogel (Ro-HEL). He spent time with the Calusa in 1566, teaching them about Christianity. While Rogel's information may contain some mistakes, it gives us an interesting glimpse of Calusa life.

According to Rogel, the Calusa believed in three different gods. The first controlled the sun, the stars, and the seasons. The second was responsible for the well-being and government of the people. The third decided who would win in battle. After learning about Christianity, the Calusa people were willing to add the Christian God to their belief system, but they weren't willing to give up own their deities.

The Calusa people told Father Rogel that each person had three souls. One soul was located in the eyes. Another was found in the reflection. And the last was in a person's shadow. The Calusa believed that when someone got very sick, it was because one of these souls had wandered off. The shaman would go out into the forest to look for this soul and herd it back toward the sick person's hut. Once the soul had returned, the shaman would build a fire in the doorway to keep the soul from getting lost again. Along with plant medicines and prayers, this was part of the Calusa healing process.

Father Rogel also recorded Calusa thoughts about death. They felt that when someone died, two of his souls entered into wild animals. When these animals died, the souls went into smaller animals, and then smaller animals, until finally the souls disappeared back into the natural world. The Calusa also believed that the eye-soul stayed with the dead person's body. Calusa people often went to burial sites to talk with dead relatives, since one of their souls was still there to listen.

Calusa beliefs about eye-souls may have tied in with their practice of **human sacrifice**. The Calusa believed that one of their gods ate human eyes. Once each year, they killed someone (probably a shipwrecked sailor) as a sacrifice to that god. Was this sacrifice supposed to help the Eater of Eyes capture the person's soul? We may never know. But we do know that stories about Calusa cannibalism are not true. The Calusa did *not* eat people. But with a god called the Eater of Eyes, it is easy to see how that rumor got started.

Rumors like these made the Spanish want to change and control Calusa beliefs. Many times Father Rogel told the Calusa chief to cut his hair, to throw away his ceremonial masks, and to have only one wife. But the chief never agreed. In fact, while the Timucua and Apalachee gave up their religions to become Christians, the Calusa never did.

The relationship between the Calusa and the Spanish came to a dangerous point one day. The Calusa put on their ceremonial masks and marched right up to the Spanish fort. The women were singing, and many Calusa people joined the worship march. When they got close to the fort, a Spanish soldier threw a spear at one of the mask wearers. It knocked him down and damaged the carved wooden mask. The Calusa knew better than to fight against Spanish guns, and they never brought their masks near the Spanish fort again. (Look ahead at figure FF on page 119 to see what a mask might have looked like.)

23

Hunting in the Water

The Calusa were excellent fishermen. In addition to hooks and lines, they also used weirs, gigs, traps, spears, and many different kinds of nets. Shallow-water nets were dragged or dipped to catch fish, shrimp, and crabs. Deep-water nets were set out for long periods of time. These nets had wooden floats at the top and shell weights at the bottom, creating a mesh wall that entangled large fish. (See figure CC.)

Since the Calusa had no hard metal, they made fishhooks from combinations of wood and bone. For shark hunting, they probably used spears. (Look back at figure V on page 75.) The Calusa and their Tequesta neighbors to the southeast hunted blacktip sharks, sharpnose sharks, and bonnethead sharks.

Historians think the Calusa used many of the same hunting techniques that some Hawaiian people use today. These Hawaiians hunt sharks from canoes by tossing out bait and by dragging shark rattles through the water. Shark rattles make a clattering noise that attracts sharks to the surface. When a shark comes up, the hunters can spear, hook, or lasso it, then kill it with wooden clubs.

Does this sound dangerous? It was, but sharks provided valuable resources. Shark meat and oil are an excellent source of protein, fat, and Vitamin A. The Calusa also got other important materials from sharks. For example, shark fins could be boiled to make glue; sharkskin was used like sandpaper for polishing shell jewelry and wooden carvings; and shark teeth made excellent drills and cutting tools. The Calusa attached these teeth to wooden handles to make knives and saws. Sometimes they embedded shark teeth in clubs to make war weapons. Shark hunting could be risky or even deadly for Calusa hunters, but the benefits outweighed the risks. Fortunately, not all of the Calusa's prey animals were so dangerous.

Fig. CC. Pulling in the nets. Drawing by Merald Clark, from *New Worlds, Old Songs: Understanding the Lives of Ancient Peoples in Southwest Florida through Archaeology,* by Charles E. Blanchard (Gainesville: IAPS Books, 1995).

A much safer food source was shellfish. The Calusa could get two pounds of meat from a large whelk. (A hamburger is only one-quarter pound of meat.) Smaller conchs, clams, oysters, scallops, and mussels were also important foods.

The Calusa pried up clams from the mud with wooden digging sticks and caught crabs from shallow waters in woven basket traps. They used whelk hammers to break off clumps of oysters and mussels and collected slow-swimming scallops, conchs, and whelks by hand.

After eating these animals, the Calusa used their shells to make tools. To make an axe, they cut a hole through the middle of the whelk shell, pushed a wooden handle through, then sharpened the tip of the shell. (Look back at figure M on page 44.) The Calusa also made whelk and clam shells into bowls, cups, spools for fishing line, beads, ear pins, net weights, awls for poking holes, vegetable choppers, and canoe anchors. Archaeologists learned about these Calusa tools by digging in the **middens** (shell trash piles) near old Calusa villages.

24

Learning from Archaeology

Calusa middens are full of discarded shells because 30 percent of Calusa foods and most of their tools came from shellfish. Sometimes the Calusa put their trash in a pile, just as people do today. Other times, the Calusa used this shell trash to build large earthworks, like hills and **canals**.

The island of Mound Key was built entirely of shells. One of the shell hills is as tall as a three-story building—34 feet high—and longer than a football field. The Calusa built their capital village on this high spot to protect their homes from flood waters. They also dug canals across their islands. These deep ditches served as canoe highways through their villages and provided excellent fishing spots close to home. (Look ahead at figure EE on page 117.)

Archaeologists have discovered hundreds of shell mounds and earthworks in Calusa territory. When they excavated these shell middens, archaeologists discovered deer-bone hairpins, whelk-shell hammers, bone beads, and lots of undecorated pottery.

However, shell mounds are not the only places we find **artifacts.** In 1896, archaeologists dug through a muddy marsh on Key Marco, an island south of Naples. These archaeologists found some amazing things, including whole fishing nets, spear throwers, animal carvings, toy canoes, and wooden masks. (See figure DD.) Underwater, these artifacts were protected from oxygen and decay. Some of the masks and carvings had been sitting there for more than a thousand years. Key Marco's people lived south of Calusa territory, long before the Spanish came to Florida. Studying the nets, tools, and masks of the Key Marco people may help us understand the art and culture of their Calusa neighbors to the north.

To learn more about Calusa slaves, shark hunting, and healing rituals, turn the page.

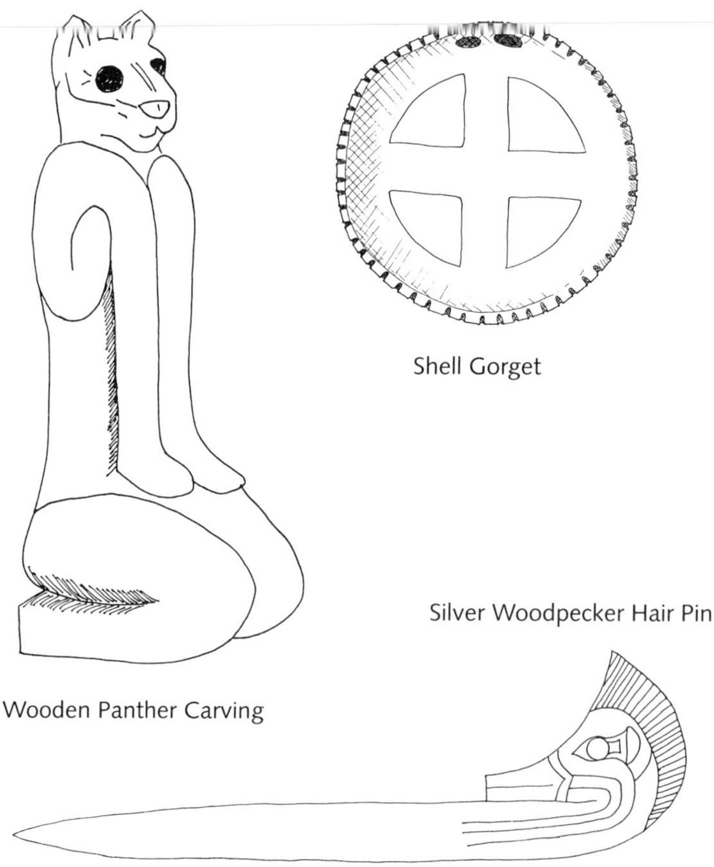

Fig. DD. Artifacts from Key Marco

25

Healing Magic

New characters in this section:

Calos (KA-los): A Calusa teenager who will become the next Calusa chief

Senquene (Sen-KEH-neh): The Calusa chief

Sheko (Sheh-KO): A thirteen-year-old escaped African slave

Vedan (VAY-den): An older Calusa man on the shark hunt

"How did you escape, Anacotima?" Just as Kidawe spoke, a huge thunder crack shook the council house. The older children tightened their arms around the little ones sitting in their laps.

Another thunderclap boomed. Then another. Lightning flashed above the broken roof. Tenerife could scarcely count to four before the next thunderclap sounded. The children's sniffling sobs filled the silence in between.

Tenerife knew he needed more than a story to ease their spirits. He needed magic. The only magic he knew was a Calusa chant he'd

---

Note: The story sections in this book are *not* fact. We know very little about the lives of real native people like Calos or Senquene. As you read, you'll learn about Tenerife's slavery among the Calusa. His memories of these events were influenced by his experiences as a slave. Just remember, some Calusa people were good, and some were bad—like the people in all cultures.

learned long ago, one that healed the body and the spirit. He began to sing it softly.

At first, he couldn't hear his own words. The sounds of the thunder and the children's crying drowned them out. But slowly, the thunder quieted, and the children began to notice his quiet chant. He sang in the Calusa language—as well as he could remember it from long ago. He had seen these words heal a badly injured boy, when everyone believed the boy would die.

Heh-heh-ya, ha-heh-ya-ha
Zemis o-a tha ya
Zemis o-a neh ya
O-ha zemis, ha-heh ya
O-ha zemis, neh ya.

Tenerife chanted the healing song four times before he saw its magic start to work. One by one, the children stopped crying. Finally, the last sniffling child took a deep breath and leaned her head against her older brother's chest. Even the thunder sounded softer, and Tenerife could hear the women chanting their own song from the birthing hut.

Tenerife changed the pitch of his chant to match the women's rhythmic music. One of the smaller children started to hum along, then another. A half-smile creased Tenerife's old brown face. He would teach the children the healing chant. Perhaps it would help Kateema, having all these young hearts and voices singing for her. He stopped chanting, and the council house fell silent. The thunder had stopped. The only sound was the women's song, which seemed soft and far away.

"I will teach you a healing chant," he said, "to help Kateema and her baby. This is powerful Calusa magic. It is not for play."

The children nodded. They understood magic and had heard stories of the powerful Calusa.

Tenerife began: "Heh-heh-ya, ha-heh-ya-ha."

The children repeated, stumbling a bit through the strange Calusa words: "Heh-heh-ya, ha-heh-ya-ha."

Tenerife chanted each line, with the older children helping the younger ones. Finally, they chanted it straight through, weaving the powerful Calusa magic around the women's songs. Tenerife could feel the magic pouring through their small bodies and into the council house. They were no longer afraid, no longer waiting for their mothers to save them. Instead, they were helping their mothers—working together to give Kateema's baby a healthy birthing. The children sang the chant again, faster this time. They shouted the last word of each line, pouring all of their old fear into this powerful healing magic.

Heh-heh-ya, ha-heh-ya-ha
Zemis o-a tha ya
Zemis o-a neh ya
O-ha zemis, ha-heh ya
O-ha zemis, neh ya.
O-ha zemis, ha-heh YA!
O-ha zemis, neh ya! O-ha zemis, neh YA!"

Tenerife held up his hands on the last "YA!" and the children fell silent. He listened as the women's chanting continued, soft in the distance.

"Anacotima," Emisu said, breathless. "How did you learn this powerful magic?"

Tenerife settled back onto his leaning bench. "I learned from the Calusa—after escaping the Spanish soldiers."

"Will you tell us the story?" Emisu asked.

Tenerife looked at the eager faces around him and nodded.

26

Slavery

"My escape began with Sheko," Tenerife said. "Without him, I would not have survived."

"Sheko, the dark-skin?" Emisu asked. "He's one of our greatest warriors."

"Yes, and my best friend. But back then, he was a boy of thirteen winters, and a slave to the Spanish priests."

"How did he save you?" Kidawe asked.

Tenerife winked at him. "I'll tell you."

I awoke in a foul-smelling place, a place full of pain, thirst, and rocking darkness. Sheko was there. He stitched the jagged wound in my leg and gave me food and water. When our ship landed on the island of Hispañola, he warned me to agree with anything the priest said. We had to gain their trust to escape them. So I nodded and smiled and said the food was so much better than what we had at home. I agreed to wear their long white smocks and even let them cut my hair.

"You let them cut your hair?" Simaru asked.

My people were dead to me—as long as I was a prisoner. For me, the cutting of my hair was a sign of mourning.

The priest thought it was a sign that I believed in his god. We told him whatever he wanted to hear. "Yes, ***Sacerdote****, I agree that there is one god. Yes, I believe that owls do not cause bad luck. I believe that—"*

"How could you say that owls don't cause bad luck?" Simaru asked.

It wasn't easy, Simaru. We know that owls cause bad luck, but the Spanish don't understand the way the world works. Sheko and I had to escape, no matter what it took.

We were prisoners at Hispañola for several moons. My leg healed, but it still pained me. Without a canoe, there was no way to escape this island of the Spanish. Some days we lit their spirit lamps and wore their smocks. Other days we carried their shiny crosses and their books.

"What's a book?" Simaru asked.

"A book is a strange thing, children. The Spanish have a powerful magic. They can capture a person's words and make them stay inside a container called a book."

"How can words stay?" Simaru said. "That's crazy."

"It is powerful magic, Simaru. They wouldn't teach us about it. It was how they talked to their god."

A howling wind turned all eyes toward the smoke hole. Tenerife smiled at the children's watchfulness. "Do not worry," he said. "It's not the sky spill."

"Anacotima," Simaru said, "tell us how you learned about the sky spill."

Sheko and I learned together. We were chosen to help teach about the Spanish god. Early one morning we sailed toward the lands of the Calusa.

"The Fierce People?" Kidawe asked.

"Yes. I told Sheko about the Calusa and their dangerous ways. We hoped for a chance to escape before we got there."

It was a stormy journey. The ship rocked and pitched in the waves. That was when it came—the sky spill. The wind howled angrily as Sheko and I struggled to tie barrels and crates to the deck. A chill rain spattered the deck as we worked.

"Ow!" Sheko shouted in surprise. He rubbed his back and leaned down to pick up a fist-sized chunk of ice from the deck. He held up the hailstone and looked at me, questioning. I shrugged and looked up at the dark sky.

Chunks of icy hail pelted the deck. Slaves and soldiers ran around, trying to find shelter from the hailstorm. Sheko and I huddled under a rolled-up sail. A windy blast howled and splashed a wave up onto the deck. We shut our eyes and clung to the sail.

For a moment, the storm quieted.

Then we heard it—the cry of a sky spill. A moment later, the sky darkened, and a torrent of water poured from the clouds. The force of the sky spill struck the boat at one end, tipping it sideways in the deep salty water. Huge waves slapped the deck. Sheko and I clung to the rolled-up sail as waves sloshed us around.

With a sickening crack, the sail broke free. We struggled to find another hand hold, but the next wave washed us off the deck and into the freezing water. Wave after wave pushed us under. But each time, Sheko and I kicked back up to the surface, coughing and choking, but alive.

Finally, the storm passed. The muscles in our legs ached. We were exhausted, and saltwater burned our eyes and throats. We climbed onto a floating barrel, shivering in our thin white smocks.

When daylight came, the ship was gone.

We were both thirsty, but we'd get no fresh water until we reached land. Sheko tried to stand up on our floating barrel so he could see further, but it spun us off with each try.

"Let's paddle to land," I suggested. "Toward the rising sun."

"Wait." He pointed to the east.

I shaded my eyes and looked across the glinting water. A dark gray fin cut the surface. We would wait.

For a day we lay clinging to the barrel, while our skin burned and our throats cracked for want of water. "Look!" Sheko said on the second morning, "Land!"

We scanned the water for sharks, then began to kick and paddle, clinging to the barrel. We paddled all day and reached land before dark. Sheko and I stumbled onto the beach, exhausted. We found some vines with large leaves and licked the drops of cool, clean water cradled on their surfaces. Then we lay down by the leafy plants and slept.

It was barely daylight when I felt something poking my chest. I looked up into several spears tipped with stingray spines—the weapons of the Matecumbe.

We couldn't speak their language, but we understood a little. We were slaves again. They gave us some water, then put us to work, searching the beach for parts of the wrecked ship.

They picked through the pieces and found jars of oil, rolls of sailcloth, containers of corn, and tools made of metal. All day and part of the next, Sheko and I worked for the Matecumbe, carrying the salvaged goods on our backs, canoeing them across salty waters, then carrying them again.

"Where are we going?" I asked a Matecumbe warrior.

When I heard his answer, I felt my throat tighten. "Calusa," he said. "Shell Island."

As we poled through the shallow canals, we saw canoes and huts everywhere. Rectangular houses sat on poles high above the water. Nearly four hundred people came out to look at us. I'd never seen so many people in one place.

The Matecumbe marched us to a large hut on a high shell mound. They made us sit with the salvaged tools and jars of oil. Mosquitoes were biting terribly, but we stayed still. Two tall men walked up. One had black paint covering most of his body. The other had dark purplish-red markings painted across his shoulders. When the second man saw the metal cross around my neck, he walked over and spoke loudly. I didn't understand then, but he was the shaman, and I was to be his slave. He took my metal cross and placed it around his own neck. The black-painted Calusa chief took Sheko to be his slave.

"Anacotima," Kidawe interrupted, "tell us how you escaped."

It didn't happen overnight, Kidawe. They never let Sheko and me work together. If Sheko was mending fishing nets, I was sent to gather medicinal plants for the shaman. If Sheko was scooping out mud to deepen the canals, I was collecting **cocci bugs** *to make red paint for the shaman's masks. Finally, we had a chance to plan together.*

"Did you hear?" Sheko asked. "The chief's heir is going on his first shark hunt, and I'll be paddling his canoe. See if you can come. We'll make a break for it."

"Meet me by the north canal when Father Sun rises again," I told him. "We'll come up with a plan." Sheko winked at me and left. The chief's heir was fifteen winters old, and he had beaten Sheko more than once. We avoided him whenever we could. But this might be our chance to escape.

Fig. EE. Calusa slaves dig a canal at Mound Key. Drawing by Merald Clark, from *New Worlds, Old Songs: Understanding the Lives of Ancient Peoples in Southwest Florida through Archaeology*, by Charles E. Blanchard (Gainesville: IAPS Books, 1995).

27

Shark Hunt

"How did you get the shaman to let you hunt?" Kidawe asked.

"I worked with him all evening, Kidawe, mixing paints for the mask he was carving. Finally, I thought of a way."

"Shaman," I said, "the mask you are carving will please the gods. It would be even more beautiful if it were polished. I could make it shine for you—if I had some sharkskin to work with. At home, we—"

"I have an idea," the shaman interrupted. "That arrogant boy, Calos, is going on a shark hunt tomorrow. Go with him. You can claim a piece of sharkskin for me." The shaman turned back to his carving. "And don't fall out of the canoe," he added. "It takes too long to train a good slave."

I nodded and continued mixing his paints. But inside I was laughing. We were going to escape!

When Father Sun rose, I jogged to the north canal to meet Sheko. My deer-fur wrap whipped around me in the chilly morning, but I barely felt the cold. Where was Sheko? I paced back and forth along the canal's edge. The small waving crabs darted about and fought as always. I waited, looking up and down the canal, but Sheko never came. I walked back slowly, afraid to return to the shaman's hut. Had our plan been discovered? I wound my way through the canals, shivering my

Fig. FF. Calusa shaman

way through the thigh-deep waters. When I got to the chief's house, I stopped underneath to listen. Calos and the chief were arguing.

"You went too far, Calos," the chief said.

"He's a stupid slave. He deserved a beating."

I held my breath. Was Sheko dead?

The chief's voice was strong. "He's my slave, Calos, and he works hard. If you beat him so hard that he can't work, I lose his services. You will not do that again."

I let my breath out quietly. Sheko was alive.

"But he's so stupid," Calos said. "The other slave is learning to speak much faster."

"Stupid or not, he's my slave, Calos. You will not beat him again. Understood?"

I took off at a jog toward the shaman's hut. They were wrong about Sheko. He wasn't stupid, he was pretending. Since they thought he couldn't understand their words, they spoke carelessly, giving away clues that would help us escape.

But how could that happen now? Sheko couldn't go on the hunt. "Shaman," I said, "my friend was beaten by Calos. I would like to take him some willow-bark tea and make **poultices** *for his bruises. May I do this?"*

"You have been paying attention to my healing plants," he said. "Good. I will teach you more in the coming days. Go on. Tend to your friend. But do not anger Calos. If he beats you, I won't get my sharkskin."

When I arrived at the chief's house, Sheko's eyes were nearly swollen shut. The dark skin of his face and stomach was patterned with purplish-black bruises. I boiled water for willow-bark tea and made a dodder-vine poultice for his eyes.

"My friend," I said in Spanish, "I think it's time you learned to speak more Calusa."

He tried to grin, but his face twisted in pain.

"Don't laugh," I said. "Listen, I'm going on the shark hunt, but you can't now. The plan is ruined."

"No," Sheko whispered. "You can still escape."

I shook my head. "I'm not leaving you here with Calos. Besides, the summer **solstice** *is coming. They'll need a sacrifice for the Eater of Eyes. Who do you think Calos will choose?"*

Sheko nodded and leaned forward to drink the pain-killing tea.

"We'll get another chance," I whispered. "Just concentrate on healing. Drink more willow-bark tea at midday for the pain. Leave

the poultices over your eyes and rest. By dark, you should be able to see clearly again. I have to go now, to prepare for the hunt."

We loaded six canoes with bone-tipped spears, wooden clubs, shark rattles, and long palmetto ropes. Gourd buckets full of smelly fish entrails went aboard last of all. Calos sat alone in his canoe, traveling light and taking the lead.

Once the canoes were clear of the island, Calos ordered me to switch to his canoe. I stepped carefully out of the longer heavier canoe into his smaller one. The lighter canoe rocked sharply as I stepped in.

"Be careful, slave!" Carlos shouted.

I braced my weak leg against the side of the canoe and paddled southwest toward the open water. Sharks always came closer to shore at night, so we watched and waited.

Fig. GG. Calos in his canoe. Drawing by Merald Clark, from *New Worlds, Old Songs: Understanding the Lives of Ancient Peoples in Southwest Florida through Archaeology,* by Charles E. Blanchard (Gainesville: IAPS Books, 1995).

Finally, someone whispered "Fin!" We all searched the darkness, straining to see for ourselves. Quietly, the men and boys tied ropes to the ends of their spears. They hung shark rattles on the outer sides of the canoes to clatter and call the sharks closer.

"There it is!" I whispered loudly, pointing west. A small fin cut the surface of the water a hundred footsteps off, then disappeared. Quietly, someone in each canoe scooped fish entrails into the water, leaving a bloody trail to draw the shark. Every man and boy stood ready, holding a tethered spear or a rope lasso. The fin came nearer, then disappeared again. We waited.

"You." Calos grabbed my shoulder and whispered roughly. "You don't hunt. Understand?"

I nodded, gripping my spear tighter. A slave couldn't hunt better than a boy who would be chief. A chilly wind blew, rippling the surface of the water. I watched as the ripples dissolved, split by a dark gray fin. "There!" I whispered.

Calos threw his spear, but it sailed harmlessly into the water. "You, slave," he said, "give me your spear and pull mine in!" He grabbed my spear, shoving me over backward. I fell hard against the side of the canoe, rocking it dangerously. "Stupid slave!" Calos said. "Pull in my spear!"

I rubbed my hurt leg as I pulled Calos's spear into the canoe. Two more men threw spears, and others scooped more entrails into the water. I stood uneasily, the rope of Calos's spear wrapped tightly around my hand so I couldn't drop it. Like everyone else, I watched and waited.

A second fin, much larger than the first, cut the water close to our canoe. Calos threw his spear, and three other men threw theirs. The shark dove, spooling out the long ropes attached to each spear. When the palm cords tightened, the canoes jerked suddenly, knocking me off balance. Several others fell too, and I heard a splash. It was Veden, one of the older men. Many hands reached into the water and hauled him out. I could hear his heavy breathing as he thanked them.

Then the ropes went slack. I looked around at the dark water. Moonlight gleamed off every ripple. We all watched and waited. The men tied their spear tethers tightly to the canoes to keep the shark from escaping.

"There it is!" Calos called. He scooped entrails into the water right next to our canoe and readied his lasso. As the shark came closer, the men pulled in their lines and tied them again, holding the shark nearby. When the animal surfaced, Calos threw his lasso. The rope fell perfectly around the shark's tailfin. Another man lassoed the shark's head, and everyone pulled the ropes tight.

The water erupted. The shark thrashed against the lassoes and spears, splashing saltwater and spray in every direction. Then the canoe rocked sharply, and Calos stumbled backward into the water.

28

Escape

"Did the shark get him?" Kidawe asked.

Calos struggled to get back in the canoe. I grabbed one of his arms and pulled as hard as I could. A man leaped into the canoe to help. The shark thrashed loudly behind us as the men clubbed it unconscious. I ignored the sounds and focused on Calos. We nearly had him in the canoe. Then his body jerked away from us and slipped under the water.

I peered at the dark surface, looking for any sign of him. Suddenly, his head and arms bobbed up. "Help me!" he sputtered. We grabbed at his blood-slick hands and struggled to pull him into the canoe. Then we heard a voice shout, "Shark!"

The man in our boat grabbed Calos by the hair and hauled him up. But not quickly enough. I saw the shark's shining black eyes as it attacked, and I could smell Calos's blood on the water. There was only one chance.

I gripped my spear tightly and aimed at the shark's bright eyes. With all of my strength, I stabbed again and again. I hardly noticed when they pulled Calos into the canoe, or when they finally took the spear from my hands. When I looked down, I saw two dead sharks, one on each side of the canoe.

The man in my canoe shook me. "Come, slave to the shaman. Tend to Calos's wounds. We must hurry. More sharks will come."

Calos's spirit had fled, but his chest moved, and his eyelids flickered. He groaned. I pressed with all my weight on the gaping wound in his right thigh, trying to stop his life's blood from flowing away. I took some crushed elderberry leaves from my hip pack and rubbed them into the injury. With luck, this might stop the bleeding.

I checked the wound. The blood had stopped pumping out. Now it was only seeping. I folded a strip of leather and used palm rope to tie it tightly over the ragged gashes. Calos's left foot was also wounded, but I ignored it, holding pressure against the leather bandage. If the heavy bleeding didn't stop, Calos would die. The other hunters tied the smaller blacktip shark to our canoe, and the larger panther shark between two others. Two hunters stood in our canoe, paddling fast, racing to save Calos's life.

By the time we reached the village, Calos's spirit had returned. His face twisted in pain as we carried him to the shaman's hut. The healer ordered everyone out, then uncovered Calos's injury. I watched and waited.

"Good work," he mumbled to me and set about cleaning the wound. "Give him some willow-bark tea. Crush some catalpa pods, enough to fill your hand. Boil it down. Give it to him in sips. It will make him sleep. There, in the yellow pot."

I made medicine while the shaman used deer ***sinew*** *and a bone needle to stitch up Calos's leg. He sprinkled more crushed elderberry leaves into the wound and whispered several chants. Then he wrapped the leg and added a few stitches to the smaller wound on Calos's foot.*

"I will see him now!" Chief Senquene's voice thundered just outside the hut.

A moment later, he pushed through the doorway and looked down at Calos. The young man tried to sit up before the chief.

"Lie down," the chief said. "Rest. You will need to dance the success of your hunt when you are healed. Two sharks, my boy, are something to dance about. I am proud of you."

Calos smiled weakly and lay back. As he shut his eyes, the chief and the shaman stepped away. "Will he live?" the chief asked.

"It is up to the gods, now," the shaman said. "I have stitched the wound and made the medicines. The slave and I will chant for him, to keep his spirit close and help him heal."

I fed medicine tea to Calos in slow sips and pretended not to listen to their words. But I could hear.

"Did they tell you?" the chief asked. "Your slave saved his life. He killed a six-footstep blacktip by himself and treated Calos's wounds. Keep him close to Calos, my friend. He may bring us the luck we need."

The chief walked up behind me. "Boy, they tell me you have worked hard to save Calos's life. Choose your trophy from the shark you killed." I looked over at the shaman and said, "The shark's skin, to polish my master's masks and carvings, to honor the gods."

The chief nodded. "You shall have it. Keep Calos alive." Then he walked out of the hut.

The shaman sat next to me, listening to the rate of Calos's breathing and the thump of his chest. He looked grave and said, "He may not survive."

I continued feeding sips of tea to Calos. What would happen if he died? I had heard of boys being killed to accompany a young chief to the spirit world. I wasn't ready for that. "He won't die, Shaman," I said. "I will chant for him, and you can call on the gods to make him strong." Together, we sang many healing chants, but the most powerful one, we chanted again and again.

Heh-heh-ya, ha-heh-ya-ha

The children chanted along with Tenerife.

Zemis o-a tha ya
Zemis o-a neh ya
O-ha zemis, ha-heh ya
O-ha zemis, neh ya.

The shaman and I were still chanting when Father Sun began to rise. I asked permission to pass my water, and the shaman nodded. "The danger is over, Tenerife. Calos will live. His leg will live. He will be chief someday." I nodded as I walked, trailing my hands along the mat-covered walls. As I stepped through the doorway, my fingers fell across a bow and quiver of arrows. I quietly took them and walked toward the chief's hut. Bags of dried sea grapes hung from the bottom of the chief's house, and I looped three bags over my shoulder while I listened. There was no sound inside. I made the quiet call of a ***whippoorwill****, over and over, hoping that Sheko would hear and waken. After a long time, he stumbled out, squinting and holding his ribs.*

I made the whippoorwill call again, and Sheko climbed down the ladder to meet me. "Come on," I said. "We're going, now."

"Tenerife, I can't run."

"Your ribs aren't broken; you'll be all right. Besides, we'll take a canoe. No one will notice."

"Are you crazy? They'll come after us. Unless—" Sheko stopped in midsentence and looked around. "We need a diversion. Go get the canoe ready. Fill a water bag. Grab a fishing line and a dip net if you can."

"What are you going to do?" I whispered.

Sheko grinned. "You'll see."

I moved stealthily through the early dawn. Normally, the women would be working already, mending nets or coiling pottery. But everyone had been up late the night before, butchering the sharks or worrying about Calos. The way was clear. I chose a smaller canoe that Sheko and I could manage alone and packed two extra paddles, a hook and line, water bags, and a pot of dried fish and oysters. I sat down in the canoe, then stood up again. Where was Sheko?

Father Sun rose higher and higher, but Sheko still didn't come. Then I smelled smoke. And not from a small cooking fire. This was a blaze, but where was it? At that moment, Sheko appeared, hobbling through the canal, holding his side. Go, he motioned. I pulled the canoe out into the water. As soon as he was aboard, I pushed my paddle hard against the shell and mud shore.

"Fire!" a voice yelled. Other shouts joined in. People stumbled out of their huts and ran toward the hut where Calos lived.

I grinned and turned around to look at Sheko. "You set Calos's house on fire?"

"Seemed fair." Sheko grinned back.

I laughed out loud. We were free.

Apalachee People

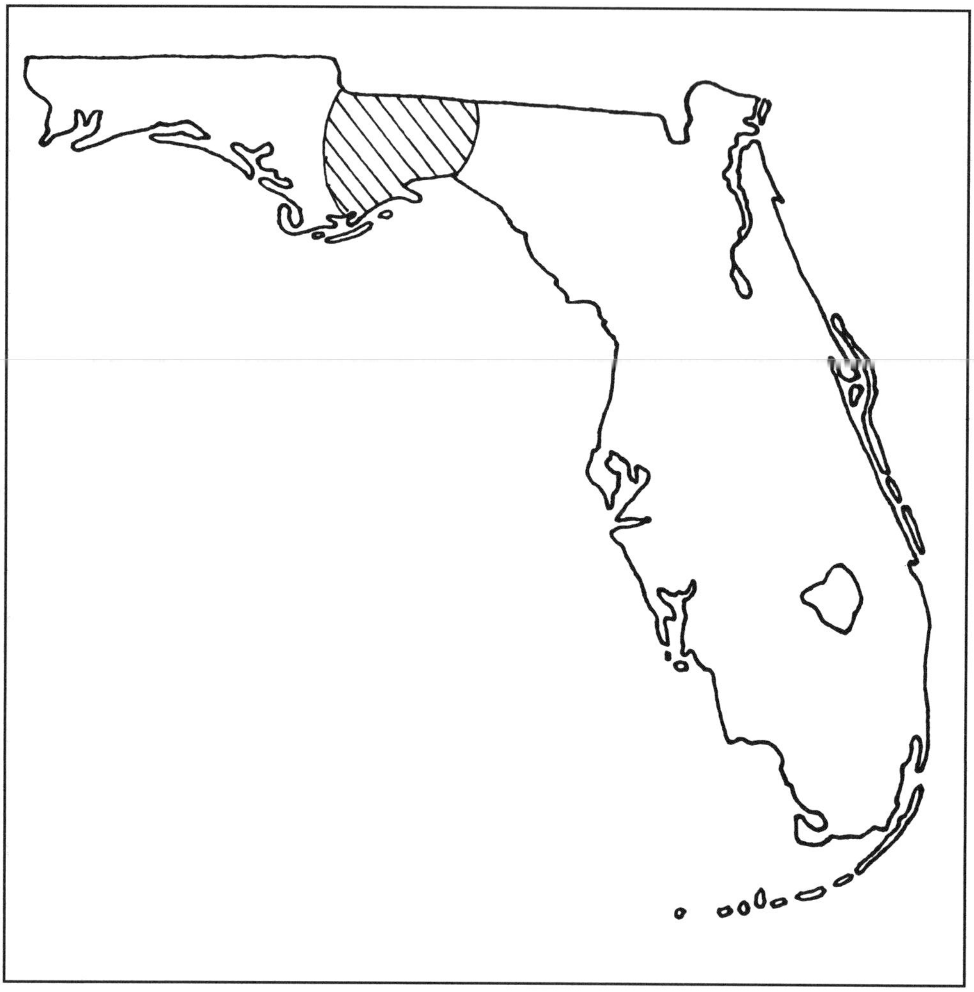

Fig. HH. Map of Apalachee territory

29

Farmers and Governments

The Apalachee (A-puh-LAH-chee) people were excellent warriors and farmers. They lived in the area where Tallahassee is today. (See figure HH.) The Apalachee chose high, dry places with good soil so they could grow plants to eat and trade. Knowing how to plant large gardens helped them produce more food, but it took a lot of time and effort. Many people had to work together to clear the fields, plant and harvest the crops, and store the food. The chief and his top advisor, the *inija*, organized work groups and settled arguments.

Crops like corn and pumpkin needed lots of rain. A drought could mean starvation for the Apalachee. They needed a powerful shaman, someone they hoped could control the weather and bring them luck. Good weather brought extra food to help their villages grow. These growing villages needed even more space and more gardens to support them. When Apalachee storehouses were full of corn, their villages became targets for attack. They needed to train their young men as warriors to protect these food resources.

Becoming farmers forced the Apalachee and their culture to grow and change. The people needed a larger population to work the fields, a larger army to protect the stored foods, and a larger government to coordinate the work forces.

This government had three levels: local chiefs, head chiefs, and **paramount chiefs**. None of the chiefs had to plant their own crops. The village planted and tended special fields just for them. Each local chief ruled one village. Along with their advisors, local chiefs organized planting, formed trade agreements with other villages, and settled arguments.

The villages located near each other often paid **tributes** of food and respect to their head chief—the next level of government. They worked on the head chief's projects too, such as building a regional council house. The head chief helped his villages work together, solved their disputes, and distributed food and seed if a village ran low. Most Apalachee families lived away from the village centers, near their gardens. These families traveled to the head chief's village for dances, ceremonies, and important celebrations.

The highest rank in the Apalachee government was the paramount chief. This man and his advisors helped settle arguments between head chiefs, developed trade relationships with faraway groups of people, and made treaties with other powerful cultures in Florida—or declared war on them. During times of peace, the leader of the village Ivitachuco became the paramount chief. During war times, the chief of Anhaica ruled.

30

Games, Trade, and War

The Apalachee governments protected their people in three ways. They played a ball game with other villages, made trade agreements, and trained warriors.

How could playing a ball game make their villages safer? The Apalachee played the ball game to bring their village good luck and good crops. This protected the people from hunger. Also, if villages were arguing, they could play the ball game instead of going to war. This sport was rough—a mix of football, soccer, and basketball—played with no protective pads. It allowed the men in these villages to compete instead of killing each other. Playing together could also have helped them solve their problems.

Villages that got along with each other also played this sport. While it was sometimes dangerous, the ball game was an exciting event that created a strong team spirit in each village. Training for this sport kept Apalachee men in good physical condition for trading, fighting, and hunting.

Hunting provided more than just meat. It could also help prevent wars. For example, the chief automatically got the furs from any bears or panthers his men hunted, along with any treasure captured during battle. He could build friendships with other chiefs by giving them these valuable furs or treasures.

Trade gave villages another good reason to be friendly. Working together, they could get things they needed or wanted, sometimes from far away. The Apalachee traded things like tools, corn, shells, and tea to get stone axes, copper jewelry, and special religious objects.

They traded with people as far away as Georgia, Alabama, and the Carolinas. The Europeans thought Apalachee chiefs ruled all of those lands and the mountains that ran through them. They even named those mountains the "Appalachians."

In addition to playing ball games and making trade agreements, Apalachee chiefs could also call on warriors to fight in battle. These men wore fierce-looking red paint on their skin and feathers in their hair. Young men became entry-level warriors, or *tascaias*, by taking one **scalp**. They moved up in the warrior ranks, to the *noroco* level, by taking three scalps. To reach the highest warrior rank, called *nicoguadca*, experienced warriors had to take ten scalps. Few men reached this level. But regardless of his rank, every Apalachee man was a capable hunter, warrior, and ball-game player.

31

Women's Jobs

Women and men led very different lives in an Apalachee village. Men wore leather loincloths, and women wore skirts made of plant cloth. Men played the ball game, while women danced at celebrations and played a game called **lacrosse**. Even their jobs were different.

Apalachee women were not chiefs or advisors, but they provided valuable resources to their people. They even invented Florida's first sports drink—*tolocano*. The Apalachee knew what a person needed to stay strong and healthy: sugar, protein, and fat. With this knowledge, the women invented *tolocano* by mixing water with powdered ingredients like groundnuts, corn, dried persimmons, and blueberries. Think of it as Groundnut-Persimmon Gatorade.

The women also ground up hickory nuts and acorns to make a nutty oil. This buttery liquid added a rich flavor to Apalachee vegetables and breads. The women wove baskets, made tools, dried gourds, and coiled clay pottery. Their clay pots and bowls were usually large, which suggests that many families cooked their meals together. Most Apalachee pottery did not have decorations, but the women sometimes added a **check stamp** or **complicated stamp** decoration. After living near the Spanish, the Apalachee began to make plates and dishes for the Spanish to use. These dishes are called Colonoware, since the Spanish were **colonists**. (See figure II.)

Apalachee women may have hunted small animals, but they depended on the men in their family for most of their meat and furs. If a woman's husband was killed in battle, she might not be able provide for all of her family's needs, so Apalachee communities set up a plan to help widows. These women could earn supplies for their families by doing community work, like cleaning the council house or sweeping the ball-game field. This was Florida's first public **welfare** system.

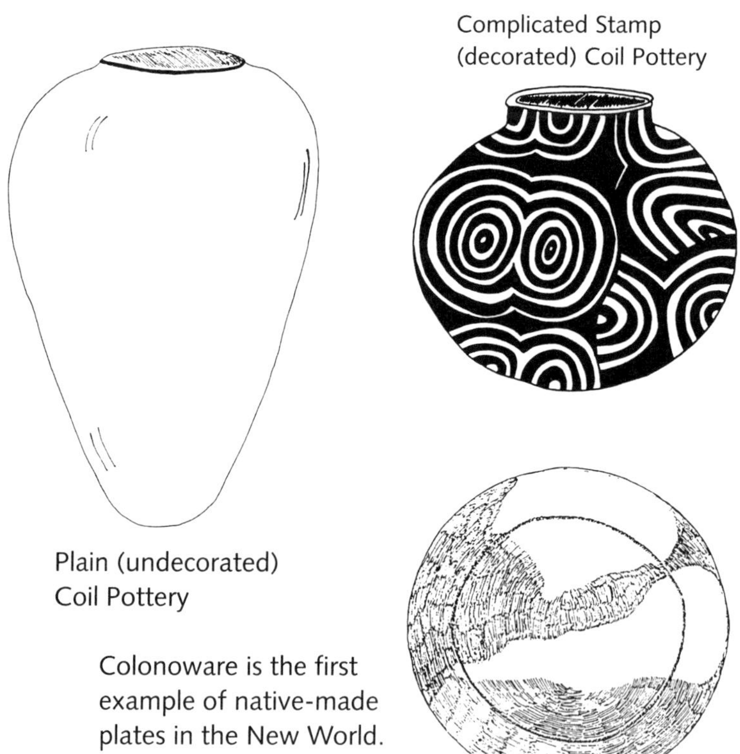

Fig. II. Apalachee pottery and Colonoware

32

The Council House

In 1656, Spanish priests built a mission church in the Tallahassee area. Many Christian Apalachee decided to move closer to the church. They lived near the village of San Luis.

As hundreds of years passed, the San Luis buildings disappeared. With hard work, archaeologists have found the exact locations of San Luis's council house, mission church, and ball-game field. Through careful digging and study, they've found pottery, stone tools, religious objects, and even human burials.

Using this knowledge, historians rebuilt the entire council house, the mission church, and other structures much as they were in Apalachee times. If you would like to explore this council house yourself, look up the San Luis Archeological Site in "Native American Places to Visit" near the end of this book.

The San Luis council house is more than 120 feet across. (That's longer than three school buses parked end to end.) This circular structure could hold more than 2,000 native people. (See figure JJ.) If you visit San Luis today, you can walk inside this giant thatched hut. You can touch the huge support logs and try to count the thousands of palm fronds in the tightly woven roof. When you enter through the low four-foot door, you'll see broad benches and

Fig. JJ. Council house, ball-game court (*lower left*), and corn fields

woven mat curtains stretching all the way around the inside wall. Each bench section has its own mat walls for privacy. These benches served as guest rooms for travelers and seating for Apalachee people attending dances, celebrations, and meetings.

You will also see an inner row of support poles and benches. The more important Apalachee families relaxed here on layers of comfortable animal furs. Near the center of the council house is a large fire pit and, above it, a hole in the ceiling that may have been thirty feet across.

Other Apalachee buildings were much smaller than the council house. Homes were usually 18–22 feet wide. These homes probably looked very much like the round, palm-thatched Timucua homes. (Look back at figure O on page 48.) Each Apalachee family had an elevated outdoor storehouse for the plant foods they harvested and collected. (See figure KK.) They may have stored meat separately in a community storehouse, so everyone could share it.

The villagers also used their ball-game field for meetings, work projects, and other community activities. There weren't many family huts at San Luis, because most families lived a mile or two away near their gardens. Keep reading to learn more about the Apalachee as Tenerife and Sheko struggle to get home.

Fig. KK. Apalachee family storage hut

33

Living Off the Land

New characters in this section:

Isa (EE-sa): The fourteen-year-old daughter of the Apalachee chief, Sava's sister

Nicoguadca (nee-ko-GUAD-kuh): The Apalachee thunder god

Pansaca (Pan-SA-ka): An Apalachee boy in the ball game

Sava (SA-va): The thirteen-year-old son of the Apalachee chief, Isa's brother. His full name is Savacola.

Ynac (EE-nak): An Apalachee boy in the ball game

Tenerife looked up through the damaged palm roof. The sky was growing lighter, and he could hear the women chanting, faster now. The baby would come soon.

"Anacotima!" The children interrupted his thoughts. "How did you and Sheko find your way home?"

Tenerife listened a moment more to the women's chant. He felt its rhythm and strength settle into his muscles. He knew that Kateema could feel it too. The beat of the women's chant gave her a rhythm for breathing and pushing, helping her baby's birth. He waited until the women paused, then began.

It was a long journey, children. One night, on the banks of the

***Tocobaga River**, we were soaked by freezing rain. We huddled under our canoe, shivering in our furs as large raindrops and small hailstones pelted the canoe bottom. We weren't far from a Tocobaga village, but we stayed away from the warmth and shelter. Who knew what the Tocobaga would do to escaped slaves?*

Maybe it didn't matter. I had already been away from home for so long. If Ashefa had promised to marry Saturiwa, what was there to go home to? I imagined miserable things all night, curled up under our canoe. I listened to the beating hail and said nothing. But Sheko knew I was thinking about her.

"Sleep, my friend," he said. "You can't win her love tonight."

I nodded. Many times, Sheko had watched me think of Ashefa. He had no words to help. So he always told me to sleep.

It was just before the Planting Moon, the coldest time of the year, and our Calusa food was running out. We paddled north to the beginning of the Tocobaga River. Then we carried our canoes over dry land to reach a new river heading northwest. We dangled our bone fishhook into the water and hid whenever we heard people. While we traveled, I spoke to Sheko in my own language, teaching him the words he would need when we reached my home.

*One day, as we floated downriver, we heard voices nearby. We paddled the canoe quietly to the bank and hid ourselves in the thick grasses and shrubs, listening. We understood some of the hunters' words. Their language was almost like Calusa. They spoke of a river up the coast called **Guacara**.*

*"We can follow it northeast—toward home!" I whispered to Sheko. He gripped my hand and smiled. We knew the journey home would take us through the lands of Saturiwa's enemies, so we camped at a lake called **Tsala,** to prepare.*

Sheko and I hid our canoe and cut saw-palmetto fronds to make a warm shelter for sleeping. We spent our first two days fishing and drying our catch over small smokeless fires. Other days, we gathered plant foods. Ashefa had taught me how to find them, even when the trees were winter-bare.

Sheko and I collected the dried berries from winged sumac trees to make a tart drink and boiled primrose roots for snacks. We cooked violet leaves and the potato-like roots from groundnut vines. We cut the leaf buds from saw palmettos and snipped the shoots from cattail grasses. When sharp winds chilled our wet hair, we ate spicy peppergrass to ward off winter colds.

But we needed travelling food. We couldn't stay hidden at Lake Tsala forever. One morning, we waded into the lake's freezing water and squished our toes through the muddy bottom.

"Ahh!" Sheko gasped when the cold water touched his skin. "Do we have to do this?"

My teeth chattered as I answered. "Not if you w-want to st- starve on the w-way home."

Sheko rolled his eyes. "Just sh-show me what to do."

When our feet touched a cattail root, we dug it out and tossed it into our palm-frond pack. By the time our packs were full, our teeth were chattering so hard we couldn't speak.

We huddled next to our fire, trying to warm up. Then we pounded the cattail roots and soaked them in a pot of water. We carefully picked out the fibers and strands and poured the water away. Only a slick white material remained. We dried it into a soft powder while Sheko practiced speaking my language.

"What will this white mess make?" he asked.

"Hard bread," I answered, "Pesolo."

"What does it taste like?"

I grinned. Sheko had never eaten hard bread before. "Oh, it's good," I said. "Just take a big bite when it's done. You'll see."

"You told him to take a big bite?" Kidawe said. "It's hard as stone!"

Old Tenerife grinned. "Sheko didn't know that."

We mixed the cattail flour with water, ashes, and crinkled red partridge berries. I picked up a blob of the sticky dough and flicked it at Sheko.

He tried to scrape the gooey mess out of his hair and yelled, "Tenerife, you're in for it!" A moment later, a glob of slimy dough smacked into my chest.

I grabbed a fish from the drying rack and flung it at Sheko, then took off running through the forest.

Sheko was even faster than I was. I'd hardly run 40 footsteps when he tackled me from behind. He rolled me onto my back and pushed a gluey blob of raw dough into my mouth.

I spit it out and sat up, laughing. But Sheko wasn't laughing. He was staring at the ground behind me. I turned to look and saw an arrow shaft, partly buried in the pine needles. Quietly, Sheko helped me up, and we jogged back to our camp. We weren't alone.

We stayed up late that cold night, shaping the sticky dough into circles, each with a hole in the middle. I took the first shift at standing guard and loaded the gooey circles into our clay pot. They baked all night until they were solid and hard.

Sheko woke me in the morning. "The pesolo." he said. "It's ruined. I nearly broke my teeth trying to eat one."

"It's hard bread," I laughed. "What did you expect? Watch this." I boiled some water and dropped the hard bread in. Slowly, it softened, and we tried a bite. Sheko made a face.

"Don't be so picky," I said. "The women would have seasoned it better, but this isn't so bad. Hard bread will last for moons. It never spoils. And look." I ran a piece of palm rope through the hole in each

piece of hard bread, stringing them up. Then I looped the string over my shoulder.

Sheko grinned and nodded. "How many of these tasteless hard breads do we have?"

"Enough for half the journey, I hope."

Sheko nodded. "Then it's time to go."

We started off the next day, leaving the safety of Lake Tsala and paddling hard toward the northwest. When we reached the coast, we stopped to gather shellfish, but didn't stay long enough to cook them. We ate them raw, feeling the oysters slide down our throats as we searched for the Guacara River.

When we heard voices, we paddled into the shallow needlerush, lying low in our canoe. The voices came closer. Their accent was strange, but I understood every word.

"Who were they?" Simaru asked.

Tenerife answered quietly. "Enemies."

34

The Challenge

"Who were they, Anacotima?"

"Allies of the **Potano**. Enemies of our chief."

"Potano," the children whispered with awe. Potano's people lived to the west. They were hated almost as much as Outina's people who lived just across the river.

"What did you do?" Kidawe asked.

"We waited until they passed, then headed back out to deeper water—away from the Guacara River. If allies of the Potano caught us, we would be slaves again—or worse."

"So you missed the river home?" asked Simaru.

"We had no choice."

We had enough hard bread to last a while longer, so we paddled northwest, up the coast. Each time we heard people nearby, we paddled close, hid our canoe, and listened. And each time I recognized their language, I knew we were still among enemies.

After several days, we saw a group of women with dip nets, pulling fish from a small weir. The women shouted at us and made motions for us to go away.

Sheko and I looked at each other and grinned. We didn't recognize a word they said.

As we paddled up the coast, we saw many boys playing a ball game. Sometimes we hid in the grassy rushes to watch them. We listened to them talking and tried to learn their words. "I wish we could play," Sheko said. "It looks like fun."

We watched a while longer then returned to our canoe. We'd heard about a river that would take us northeast, the Aucilla. It wouldn't take us all the way home, but it would be a good start.

After paddling up the Aucilla River for two days, we decided to stop and gather more food. We hadn't seen or heard anyone and thought we could light a fire without attracting any attention. We were wrong.

We were sitting by our fire, drying the fish we'd caught that day, when the Challenger walked into our camp.

Fig. LL. Savacola the Challenger

"The what?" Kidawe asked.

"The Challenger, Tenerife repeated.

He was a boy—only a little older than I was. His face was painted red with clay, and his body was striped black and red. He had a raccoon tail tied to his hair and another to the back of his loincloth. This strange boy walked right up to our fire and made a hands-open sign of friendship. We nodded cautiously, and he sat before us, rubbing his painted arms to warm himself. He spoke to us in his language, but we understood only a little. He seemed to be asking where we were from. I gestured far to the northeast, many days' travel from there.

He cocked his head, seeming to listen to my words. Then suddenly, he smiled.

"Do you play the ball game?" He was speaking my language! He spoke it oddly, like the people we had seen near the Guacara River. I swallowed hard. Was he enemy or friend?

Either way, I had to answer him. I reached back for my bow, trying to make it look like I was stretching. He was waiting for an answer.

"Do you mean the game where you kick the small ball?" I asked.

He nodded and smiled.

"No, we've never played," I answered carefully. His smile faded, and I tightened my grip on the bow.

"It doesn't matter," he said. "We're challenging the Yustaga. I hoped you could play for us. Many of our boys are ill with fever."

I breathed out slowly. This boy wasn't our enemy. Sheko nodded his agreement, and I relaxed my grip on the bow.

"I'm Tenerife," I said, pointing to my chest. Then I pointed to my right. "This is Sheko."

The boy tapped his own painted chest and said "Savacola." I handed him a piece of dried fish. "Quoso," he said in my language—thanks.

"Sava," Sheko said. "Why are you dressed like a raccoon?" Sheko spoke slowly, practicing my language.

"I'm the Challenger," Sava answered. "I'm going to challenge the Yustaga boys to an early ball game, to ask the thunder god for rain during the planting. They won't beat us again. Our boys are growing, and our men have beaten Yustaga in battle since the last game. We will win."

"Yustaga!" I said, suddenly understanding. "The ones who speak my language strangely? You fight them?"

Sava nodded. "Yes, we beat them. Do you fight them too?"

"We fight the Outina and the Potano," I said. "Cousins to the Yustaga."

"Enemies of my enemies," Sava said smiling. He gripped our hands tightly. "Friends of my friends, you must travel with me. Come to Ivitachuco. We are raising a ball post. It's a time of celebration. You will be welcomed."

I thought for a moment. If Sava's people hated the Yustaga, they might help us get around them on our journey home. I looked at Sheko, and he nodded. "It's a deal, Sava," I said. "Let's get some sleep. Tomorrow we all challenge the Yustaga."

We approached the Yustaga village before midday. The three of us stopped high on a hill, where the people of Yustaga could see us. Sava shook a pole topped with shiny jingling bells. He handed shell bracelets to Sheko and me, motioning for us to shake them as well. The three of us stood at the top of the hill, rattling the shells and metal bells until a boy came out from the Yustaga village. He wore a long red matchcoat and had a deer tail tied into his hair. In one hand, he held a long flexible pole.

*"**Honoso**!" he shouted. "Honoso!" Then he shook the pole, jingling the shells tied to its top.*

*"They accept!" Sava whispered. He leaped in the air. "Four days from now!" He shouted to the boy at the village. "Fifty boys to a team! **Nita**!" he*

shouted. "Nita! Nita!" Then we turned and jogged west, toward the lands of the Apalachee.

When we camped, Sava got out his ball and taught us the rules of the ball game. We practiced kicking the ball back and forth and leaping high to grab it in the air.

"Some kids were playing this to the south," Sheko said. "It looked fun."

"It can be," Sava answered, "but it's dangerous too. With 100 players on the ball field, you can end up at the bottom of a huge pile-up. I've seen players break arms and legs. But that hardly ever happens in the boys' games."

"Hardly ever?" Sheko asked.

Sava laughed. "It hasn't happened in a long time, anyway."

"Why do the men play, if it's so dangerous?"

"The best players don't have to plant or harvest."

"Corn?" I asked. "Your village grows corn?"

Sava nodded. "Of course."

"We haven't had corn in moons! The Calusa don't grow it."

Sava's eyes widened. "You lived with the Calusa? But they sacrifice travelers."

Sheko grinned. "We escaped."

Sava added wood to the fire. "That's a story I'd like to hear."

35

Meeting the Chief

"What were the Apalachee like?" Kidawe asked. "Did you get to meet their chief?"

"I did," Tenerife answered.

We paddled our canoe west across the Aucilla River and hid it in a tangle of willow trees. As we approached Sava's village, he began shaking his metal bells and calling out to his people. Sheko and I added the jingling music of the shell bracelets. By the time we reached their council house, many people had come out to meet us. I nudged Sheko. "See the feathers in that one's hair? I bet he's the chief." Sheko nodded, and we stood silent.

The chief walked toward us. "Hello, my son." Sheko and I looked at each other. Sava was the son of a chief? The chief gripped Sava's hand and continued, "I am glad the Yustaga accepted your challenge. Who have you brought from the forest?"

"Travelers, Father, enemies of the Yustaga, friends of the Apalachee. This is Tenerife, of the far east coast, and Sheko, from across the great water." We nodded to the chief when Sava spoke our names. "They were captured by the Calusa, Father, and escaped to tell the story."

The chief stepped toward us. "You will find food and rest in the council house. Tonight you will tell your stories to the people. Now, Sava, we must prepare for the ball game."

Sheko and I did as the chief said. We bathed with water from a large clay pot. Sheko handed me a shell comb for the tangles in my hair.

I turned the comb over in my hand. It looked like the one Saturiwa had given Ashefa. I closed my eyes and tried to imagine her face. No matter how hard I tried, I couldn't do it. Had she promised herself to Saturiwa? Is that why I couldn't remember what she looked like?

We ate dried venison and a porridge made of hominy corn and dried blueberries. Sheko said it was delicious, but I could barely taste it. What would I do if Ashefa had promised to marry Saturiwa? But maybe she hadn't. I could bring her a gift, something to show that I loved her. Something to show her I could make a good husband. But I didn't have even a deerskin for her. I bit my bottom lip and tried to think. What could I bring her?

I felt Sheko's hand on my shoulder. "I know," I said. "I can't win her love today. I should sleep."

We awoke to the sounds of many people. Sava's head poked through the curtain of deerskin that blocked off our sleeping area. "Wake, my friends. It's time to tell your stories to the people."

I rubbed my eyes and asked, "How many people?"

Sava winked. "All of them."

I sat up slowly, nudging Sheko. "Wake up. They want us." We sipped water from a nearby gourd and pushed the deerskin curtain aside. Hundreds of people stared at us as we stumbled from our sleeping area. Hundreds.

I felt the thumping in my chest quicken. "How many?" I whispered to Sheko.

"Six hundred, eight hundred, maybe."

I took a deep breath and stepped up to Sava's right side. Sheko stepped up to his left. The three of us walked toward the chief. He was sitting on a high platform near the center of the council house.

"Welcome, boys." The chief spoke in my language. "Sava tells me you have escaped the Calusa. Tell us the tale, friends of our friends. Most of us do not speak your tongue, so Sava will translate your story."

He gestured for us to climb up on a nearby platform. I looked around at the hundreds of faces—old faces with white hair; small round faces, babies in their mother's arms, and warriors with faces painted red and black. Each face was proud and strong. Finally, my eyes rested on a girl's face. She reminded me so much of Ashefa. That's where my story would start.

I looked out at the crowd once again. There were so many people. I opened my mouth to speak, but no sound came out.

"You were afraid to tell stories?" Simaru asked. "But you're a storyteller!"

"I wasn't, back then. I was a boy, just like you. I'd never seen that many people before, and they were all staring at me."

"What did you do?" Emisu asked.

I swallowed hard and tried to speak again. My hands trembled, and I felt the racing in my chest. Sheko stepped up onto the platform with me.

"You can do it," he whispered.

I nodded and took another deep breath. "I can do it," I said to myself. "I can do it." I thought about Ashefa. Suddenly, I could remember her face. I could do it for her. I stood as tall as I could and spoke loudly so all could hear. "There was a girl in my village," I said, "a girl so kind and beautiful, I can't imagine living without her." I talked until I was nearly hoarse. Two girls brought tea to Sava and me, to wet our throats for the long night of storytelling.

I told the tale up until the moment I was shot. Then Sheko took over. He told about his terrible journey across the Great Water and his time with the Spanish. The people listened as he described our escape from the sky spill and his life with Chief Senquene and Calos. It was well into the night when I began to speak again. I told about the shark hunt and sang the Calusa healing chant. Together, Sheko and I described our escape and journey up the coast. I told of our desire to return home, my hope to win Ashefa's love, and the enemies we would face along the way.

When we finished our tale, the chief stood before the people. "These are brave boys," he said. "They deserve to go home. But like Nicoguadca, the thunder god, they must complete three tasks to prove their worth."

Sheko and I looked at each other. What did he mean?

"First, they must plant the lead ball-player's field. This will earn them food and tools for the journey home. Second, they must help my son beat the Yustaga in his first ball game. If they win, they will earn a guide and protector on their journey home. Third, each must score a goal during the game to earn a pair of silver ear spools." The chief showed us small silver disks carved with delicate designs front and back. Sheko's eyes widened and the chief winked at us. "They might just win a young girl's heart."

Fig. MM. Silver ear spools

Suddenly, all the men and boys howled like wolves. The noise was deafening. Howls bounced off the palm-frond roof and echoed through the council house. Sava howled along with the others. Outside, the dogs of the village barked and yelped. Sheko's eyes looked large and scared. I felt my chest thumping wildly. We turned and stood with our backs together; prepared for an attack.

Finally, Sava laughed. "They're not attacking you, my friends. They're cheering for you. Join them in the howl!"

I had never howled before, but I did then. Sheko joined me, and we howled out our fear and nervous energy. Many boys worked their way toward us through the crowd to congratulate us for joining their team. Slowly, people began to file out of the council house.

Finally, only Sheko, Sava, and I remained near the central fire. I looked up at the palm roof of the council house, far larger than the one I remembered from home. Home was so far away.

I sat down hard on the floor.

"What is it?" Sheko asked.

"It's impossible," I said. "Planting a whole field and winning a game we've never played before. When are we supposed to practice? It can't be done."

"Who thought you could kill a six-footstep shark?" Sheko asked. "Who would have guessed I'd escape the Spanish?"

"My father believes you can do it," Sava said. "It won't be easy, but he thinks you can help win the ball game. Even though it's just a boy's game, winning is important. It will bring rain for the crops and help us in our next battle against Yustaga."

I nodded at Sava. "We'll try."

36

Earning a Way Home

"Did you do it, Anacotima?" Emisu asked. "Did you pass the tests?"

We did our best, Emisu.

The next day we hardly had time to think. The old men and women woke us before dawn. They taught us the layout of the fields, how deep to plant the corn seeds, and where the pumpkins, squash, and sunflowers would go in.

Kidawe interrupted. "Didn't they plant beans, Anacotima?"

Emisu elbowed him. "You put the beans in after the corn's been growing a while, remember?"

Kidawe grinned. "Oh, yeah."

The old men and women loaded us down with heavy bags of soaked corn kernels, pumpkin seeds, squash seeds, and sunflower seeds. We toted the seed bags over our shoulders and carried shell hoes and digging sticks in our hands. Heavy bags of drinking water hung down our backs attached to ***tumplines*** *across our foreheads. We staggered under our loads as the old men and women cackled.*

"Why were they laughing, Anacotima?"

"Just having fun with us, I think. We didn't care. We had work to do."

The ball-player's field seemed to go on forever. I took a deep breath and looked across the reddish-orange soil. "Where do we start?" I asked. "It's so big."

"I've got it," Sheko said. "Let's make it a race. I'll start hoeing at the far end. You start hoeing here. Whoever has hoed more when we meet in the middle gets the back of the canoe on the trip home."

I thought about it. The paddler in the back did less work. He spent most of his time steering. If the back person was really sneaky, he could relax for a nap while the front person did all the work. I grinned. "It's a bet."

"Don't start until I get there!" Sheko called, jogging to the end of the field. "Okay, go!"

I broke up the hard red clay with my shell hoe and raked it into a hill one-footstep across. Then I leaped ahead to make another hill. Hoe and rake, hoe and rake, hoe and rake. Sheko was moving just as fast as I was. When we got close to the middle, I dug into the ground as hard as I could. Hoe and rake, hoe and rake, hoe and—

"Done!" Sheko called out, right next to me. He was still raking up his last hill and finished exactly when I did.

"Who won?" he asked, breathing heavily. We counted hills. It was an exact tie.

"Hello!" We heard voices calling to us from the edge of the field. "Hello!" We jogged over, covered in dusty red clay and dripping sweat in the cool spring air. Two girls waited at the edge of the field to hand us bowls of spiced grits and venison. While we scooped grits into our mouths, they giggled, refilled our water bags, and walked off.

Sheko grinned. "That one with the purple beads is cute."

I rolled my eyes. "No time to think about that. We've got a field to plant. Want to race again? Same bet?"

"I'll beat you this time," Sheko said. "You want corn or the squashes and sunflowers?"

I took the corn. There was more space to plant, but I wouldn't have to worry about planting three different sections of the field.

"Go!" I shouted. In each hill, I poked four holes with a digging stick. Then I dropped a seed in each hole, covered them up, and moved to the next hill. Hole, hole, hole, hole, seed, seed, seed, seed, cover it all. Hole, hole, hole, hole, seed, seed, seed, seed, cover it all. I remembered a planting song we had made up at home, and I started chanting it while I worked. Time passed as I chanted the song again and again. Father Sun crossed the sky and began to set. Hole, hole, hole, hole, seed, seed, seed, seed, cover it all. The work went on and on and on.

Fig. NN. Sheko planting, with a shell hoe and digging stick

"Done!" I looked up. Sheko was standing at the far side of the field with his digging stick high in the air.

He laughed aloud. "I hope you like the front of the canoe, my friend!"

I took a deep breath as he walked toward me. Maybe corn hadn't been the smartest choice.

"Give me some seeds," Sheko said. "We'll finish the corn together."

As Father Sun set, we finished the eastern end of the field. We lay back on the rich red earth, exhausted. The first stars of the evening glowed above.

Sava's face appeared over us. "Why are you lying on the ground, my friends? A feast awaits you at the council house!" We got up slowly and gathered the tools and empty seed bags. As we walked, we tried to dust the clay from our skin. Reddish-orange powder tinged my fingernails and made my eyes itch. I tried to spit the taste of clay from my mouth. I just wanted to bathe and sleep, but that wasn't going to happen.

The sound of music and the flicker of leaping firelight reached us far out in the field. As we approached, we found the council house filled with singing and dancing.

I shouted so Sava could hear, "What's going on?"

"Tomorrow's the raising of the ball post!" he said. "Tonight, the entire village will celebrate. Every woman will join the celebration, to bring us good luck in the games!"

Sheko and I sat at the edge of our compartment in the council house, watching the dancing. Men and women sang and played bone flutes and log drums. The dancers wore shells that jingled as they leaped and twirled. The girls from that morning brought us bowls of raccoon stew with thick corn bread.

We smiled our thanks, and Sheko tried to speak to them, using a mix of Apalachee words and my language. One girl shook her head, not understanding. But the other one, the girl with the purple beads, smiled and answered Sheko's question. "We're not dancing because we're not of age yet. Only the men and women dance the ball post. But the young people have a dance of their own."

Sheko smiled at her. "You speak the Yustaga words. What is your name?"

"I am Isa, sister to Sava, daughter of the chief."

Sheko smiled even bigger. "Did you know that 'Isa' means 'beautiful' in this language?"

She shook her head. "It's not a word used in games or battle. That's all we talk to the Yustaga about. Would you two like to come to the dance?"

I smiled and shook my head. "My thanks, Isa, but I just want a bath and some rest."

"Speak for yourself," Sheko said. "I'd love to go."

Isa smiled and took Sheko's hand. "Follow us, you can both bathe in my father's hut. Tenerife can sleep there too."

Sheko finished bathing quickly and headed out the doorway. When he turned to say goodbye, I whispered, "Tell me about it tomorrow!"

37

Playing the Ball Game

"What about the ball game, Anacotima?" Kidawe asked. "Did you make a goal? Did you win?"

We spent the next morning raising the ball post and attaching an old eagle's nest to the top. Then Sava shimmied up and placed a stuffed eagle hide in the nest. It looked like a living eagle was sitting up there, watching us. Afterward, we feasted and slept. It would be a long night. The Apalachee woke us at dusk and took us to the ball court. We sat with the other boys on log benches. The chief was just behind us on a bench of his own. The smoke from his clay pipe swirled around us.

The whole team would wait together, in case the Yustaga showed up early. Sava used the time well, teaching us the strategies of the game, things we could do to bring good luck, and ways to protect ourselves. "Be careful," he said. "We won our last battle against the Yustaga. They may be looking for a fight."

All night, Sava walked up and down the long line of benches, speaking with tired boys, encouraging them or helping them with a strategy. "It's too bad Sava is the chief's son," I whispered to Sheko. "He would've made a good chief."

As Father Sun began to rise, the women braided our hair behind our heads and painted our skin black. Ivitachuco's totem animal was the black bear. During the game, we would all wear black, to ask the bear for strength in the game. "Nita" was the Apalachee word for "bear." That would be our cheer. Sava led the old men over and told us they had dreamed of good ***omens****. Then the old dreamers shared stories of great ball games from their younger days. Women brought a rich broth of deer meat for the old men. My stomach growled as I waited for mine, but a thin corn gruel was all the players were allowed to eat.*

Savacola had us all practice sprinting fast, kicking the ball, and jumping high. We were all tired when he sat us down to drink cassina, sipping slowly for energy. The women sang, dancing around the ball post in a tight circle: Step, step, twirl, step. Step, step, twirl, step. The men made a larger circle around them, dancing along but leaping at the end of each set: Step, step, twirl, leap. Step, step, twirl, leap. On the fourth beat, the men howled like wolves, and the dogs in the village barked along. Step, step, twirl, leap and howl!

Fig. OO. Tenerife and Sheko practice for the ball game

On it went, until Father Sun rose high in the sky, and the Yustaga team walked up to the ball court. When they arrived, the Apalachee men howled together. It was a terrifying noise, and the Yustaga howled back. Dogs barked wildly. For a moment, I thought we would have a battle instead of a game.

Then, in an instant, all was quiet. We walked out onto the field, fifty of us in black and fifty of the Yustaga boys painted reddish-brown. The deer, honoso, was their village's totem animal, so they were painted to match, hoping to be as fast and agile as their totem. While the teams readied themselves, hundreds of Apalachee and Yustaga families settled in to watch the match. My stomach growled as I smelled picnics of roasted venison.

Fig. PP. Picnic before the ball game. Drawing by Merald Clark, from *New Worlds, Old Songs: Understanding the Lives of Ancient Peoples in Southwest Florida through Archaeology,* by Charles E. Blanchard (Gainesville: IAPS Books, 1995).

Everyone placed bets. They bet on who would win, what the final score would be, and who would make the most goals. Some of the Yustaga called over to the Apalachee families. "Haven't your boys grown at all since last year?" one woman called.

"It's going to be a long walk home after you lose!" an Apalachee man hollered back.

I tried to ignore them. These people could gamble and argue all they wanted. I wasn't playing for them. I was playing for Ashefa.

A sharp whistle started the game. I looked closely at the Yustaga captain. He was taller than Sava, so he would probably get the ball. An Apalachee referee threw a small leather ball high into the air. Sava leaped up to catch it, but the taller boy got it first and dodged to the left. Sheko dived straight at him, knocking the ball from his hand. Sava scooped it up and held it in his mouth. He ran almost twenty footsteps before a Yustaga boy tackled him. An old man from each village blew a bone whistle, stopping the play.

Sava was breathing heavily when the last boy was pulled off him, but he still held the ball tightly in his mouth. The Yustaga referee took the ball and gestured for Sava and his tackler to face off. He threw the ball high into the air and backed away. Sava leaped, grabbed it, and shoved the ball in his mouth. He dodged around Yustaga players, running toward the ball post. I ran along beside him, blocking the tacklers. Sheko sprinted ahead just as a Yustaga boy plowed into my back. Sava spit the ball out and kicked it to Sheko. I got up in time to see Sheko punt the ball hard toward the post.

"Thwack!" Sheko had earned his silver ear spools.

"One point for Ivitachuco," the referees called out. "Scorer, line up for the jump!"

Players slapped Sheko on the back as he jogged to the starting point. The other team's captain was much taller, but Sheko leaped anyway.

Three Apalachee boys tackled the Yustaga captain as he caught the ball. He passed it to a teammate who sprinted down the field. I've never seen anyone run so fast. He kicked the ball high and hard. It went in the eagle's nest!

"An eagle goal. Two points for Yustaga!"

"Who won, Anacotima?" Kidawe interrupted.

It was a long game, Kidawe. Neither team could hold the lead. As soon as we scored, they scored too. The more tired the players got, the more mistakes they made. There were more kicks at the post, but we hit it less often. When we finally took a break, the score was 10–9, their favor. Only one point to go, and I still hadn't scored.

We all sat on the benches, exhausted. Women poured cool water over us and fed us sips of cassina. The chief told us how much he believed in us. He reminded us that our winning would bring rain for the crops. I blinked sweat out of my eyes and took a deep breath. Around us, Apalachee families started chanting "Nita, nita, nita, nita, nita!"

I took another deep breath. It felt as if some of their energy was pouring into my body. The other players seemed to feel it too. The referees blew their bone whistles, and we jogged back onto the field.

Sava spoke to the players. "This is our chance to win," he said. "Ynac, I want you to jump. Get that ball! Launch it to Sheko. He's our fastest runner. Sheko, look for me or Tenerife or Pansaca. We'll get close to the post. We've got to try for an eagle goal. We can win in one shot if we make it. Everyone else, block the Yustaga. Keep them away from us. We can do this," he said. "I believe in you."

"Ni-ta!" Ynac shouted. "Nita, nita, nita!" The whole team started the chant and kept it up as the old Yustaga referee tossed the ball high between Ynac and the Yustaga captain. They both leaped, swatting at the ball. The Yustaga captain tipped it, but Ynac got a tight hold on it.

He pitched the ball to Sheko, who dodged away from the rush of people. Sheko crammed the ball into his mouth and took off. He moved like a deer, leaping and diving through a wall of Yustaga players.

I sprinted ahead as fast as I could. The ball zoomed over my head, toward Sava on my left. It fell short, but Sava scooped it up and kept running. He cut across the field in front of me, and I sprinted alongside, blocking Yustaga attackers. My chest thumped wildly as I ran. When Sava dodged to the left, a Yustaga boy slid by me and grabbed at him. At the last moment, Sava spit the ball out and kicked it forward to Pansaca. The Apalachee boy leaped into a faster run, with me and the entire Yustaga team on his heels. Several Apalachee boys pushed up beside me. "Run!" they shouted. "We'll guard him."

I took off for the ball post, pulling farther and farther ahead. I glanced back and saw Pansaca trying to dodge the army of boys closing in on him. "Nita!" I shouted.

Even though Pansaca couldn't see me, he launched the ball in my direction. It went over my head, and I tripped backward, trying to catch it. As I struggled up, I saw a wave of brown and black bodies thundering toward me.

I shoved the ball in my mouth and lunged forward. I dodged left and right, leaping over fallen players to reach the ball post.

Suddenly, my head jerked back. A Yustaga player had grabbed my short braid. I held the ball tightly with my teeth and struggled to pull away. My head jerked back again. Then Sava blitzed by me, tackling the Yustaga. I was free. I spit out the ball and kicked it as hard as I could. It arched high above the post and dropped right into the eagle's nest.

"Eagle goal," the referees called. "Two points. Ivitachuco wins!"

The army of boys crashed into me and over me. I curled up like a turtle, with my head, arms, and legs tucked close to my belly. Toes gouged my ribs, and hands pulled my hair, but my eyes and belly were safe.

It took a long time for the referees to undo the pile-up. I could barely breathe at the bottom, but we had won. We'd earned food and tools for the journey home, a guide and guard, and the silver ear spools. I couldn't wait to give them to Ashefa.

"What happened next, Anacotima?" Kidawe asked.

"The Apalachee chief kept his word," Tenerife said. "Sava and a *Noroco* warrior traveled home with us. Sheko did make me sit in the front of the canoe for the entire journey. But I asked my uncle to adopt him anyway. We became true brothers."

"What about Ashefa?" Emsiu asked. "Was she still accepting Saturiwa's gifts?"

"Not since I had disappeared. Ashefa explained it to me. She'd only accepted his gifts to turn his attention away from me. I was so worried about losing her, and all the time she was thinking about me. She said she'd always known I would come back to her."

"How did she know?" Emisu asked.

"The shaman told her that someday she would marry me. Somehow, he knew."

For a moment, the children were silent, wondering what secrets the shaman could share with them.

"Tenerife!" a woman's voice called from outside. "We need you."

38

Kateema's Baby

Ashefa ducked through the doorway of the council house and walked quickly to her husband. "The baby won't come," she whispered. "Kateema is weakening. We need the shaman. Can you take some of the boys to search for him?"

"Anacotima," Emisu and Simaru said, "we'll go."

Tenerife shook his head. "Kateema is weak. She may not be able to wait until we find the Shaman. I think it is time to try the Calusa magic, to strengthen her baby's spirit and call it into this world. I cannot do it alone, children. Even the smallest of you will have to help."

"We can do it, Anacotima."

"We're not that small."

"It worked before."

"Then take a deep breath, children, and we'll try. Ashefa, take the girls into the birthing hut with you. The closer they are to Kateema and her baby, the better. Boys, you'll stand just outside the door with me. When I give the cue, we will chant and let the Calusa magic pour through us and into Kateema and her baby."

The children followed Tenerife and Ashefa out of the council house. In the early dawn, they walked to the birthing hut. The girls filed quietly inside, and the boys stood near the doorway with Tenerife.

"On the count of four," Tenerife said, "in time with the women's chant. One, two, three, four."

They began together, chanting with clear, clean words. No voices stumbled or sang out of tune. Tenerife could feel the power of the chant. The magic was working.

Heh-heh-ya, ha-heh-ya-ha
Zemis o-a tha ya
Zemis o-a neh ya
O-ha zemis, ha-heh ya
O-ha zemis, neh ya.

Kateema's breathing came louder, and the children chanted faster.

Heh-heh-ya, ha-heh-ya-ha
Zemis o-a tha ya

Her pains were coming every two lines now. As the children chanted faster, the baby seemed to push toward being born.

Zemis o-a neh ya
O-ha zemis, ha-heh ya
O-ha zemis, neh ya.

As Kateema struggled to have her baby, the children's voices got louder, they shouted the last word of every line, trying to give Kateema strength with their voices.

Heh-heh-ya, ha-heh-ya-HA!
Zemis o-a tha YA!
Zemis o-a neh YA!
O-ha zemis, ha-heh YA!
O-ha zemis, neh YA!

On the last "YA!" Kateema cried out. Tenerife waited in the

silence, hoping for the best. Finally, a baby cried. Women and girls inside the hut laughed aloud. "It's a boy," Ashefa called. "He's healthy. Kateema is all right too."

"Thank you for the news, my wife." The muscles in Tenerife's legs felt suddenly tired, but he was happy. Sheko would return to find his daughter and her baby alive and healthy.

Ashefa poked her head out of the women's hut. "These children have done a great work, Tenerife. Will you go to our hut and bring them some food and drink?"

Emisu stepped up. "No, Ashefa, it's Anacotima who has done the great work. He taught us the magic. We'll prepare the food."

Tenerife watched the children jog off to their huts, arguing about what foods each would bring. Father Sun was just cresting over the treetops.

"Ashefa," he said. "Father Sun is nearly up."

She reached to hold his hand. "Let's greet him together. There's much to give thanks for today."

Europeans

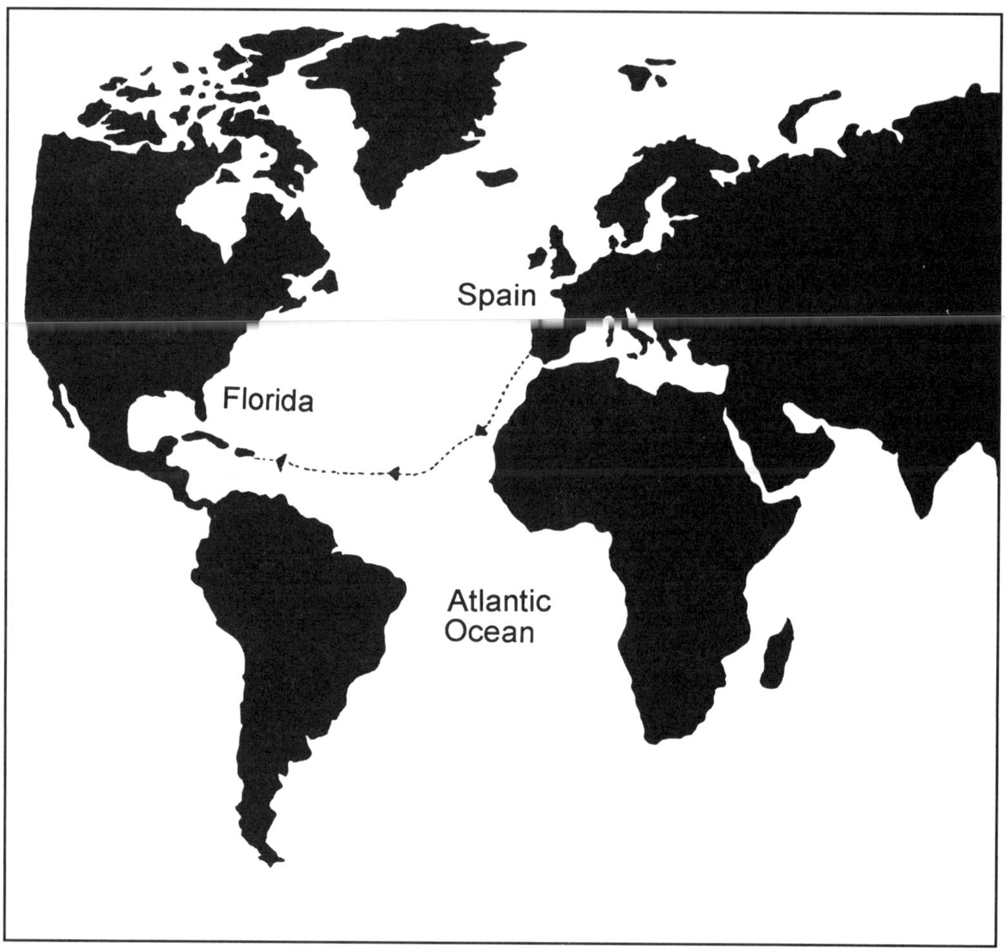

Fig. QQ. Map of Columbus's trip to the New World

39

Who Came to the New World?

To get a clear picture of native life in early Florida, we also need to learn about the Europeans who came to the New World. Who were they? Why did they come to Florida? And how did they affect the native cultures living there?

We learn the answers to these questions by reading old European letters, journals, and documents. These give us information about Florida's Indians and about the English, French, and Spanish people who interacted with them. The European cultures were never united into one group. They spoke different languages, practiced different religions, and sometimes fought wars with each other.

Europeans who came to the New World can be described as explorers, soldiers, priests, government officials, or **entrepreneurs**. The first Europeans to arrive in the New World were probably explorers from **Scandinavia**. However, it was Spanish explorers who put the New World on Europe's map. In 1492, when Spain sent Christopher **Columbus** on his famous voyage, Europeans were hoping to discover a shorter path to the East Indies, near China. Instead, Columbus discovered the Americas and opened the door to European colonization. (See figure QQ.)

Twenty-one years passed before Spain's next official visit to Florida. During these years, many European pirates and **slavers** sailed to the New World. In 1513, when Ponce de León led his official expedition to Florida, he met Indians who understood some Spanish. They might have learned this language from pirates and slavers who had already visited Florida.

Ponce de León and all European soldiers had two main tasks: first, to map the New World, and, second, to make it safe for other Europeans. Soldiers explored rivers, built forts, contacted native chiefs, and chose spots for future towns.

Priests also began arriving in Florida to teach native people about Christianity. These priests were unpopular in many villages because they told the native people to change their ways and beliefs. Some priests were killed, and many others suffered great hardships.

The growing mix of Spanish people living in Florida needed a local government. Spain sent government officials to settle arguments between the soldiers and the priests, decide where cattle ranches would be, and help find shipwrecked sailors.

The entrepreneurs arrived next, hoping to make money in the New World. These entrepreneurs became fishermen, farmers, ranchers, slavers, or government officials. (See figure RR for tools the Spanish used in early Florida.)

The Africans were another group of newcomers to Florida. Many were brought to the New World as slaves and forced to work for the Europeans. Some slaves managed to escape and joined native villages. Others remained slaves all of their lives. A few Africans came to the New World as free colonists, like the Europeans did.

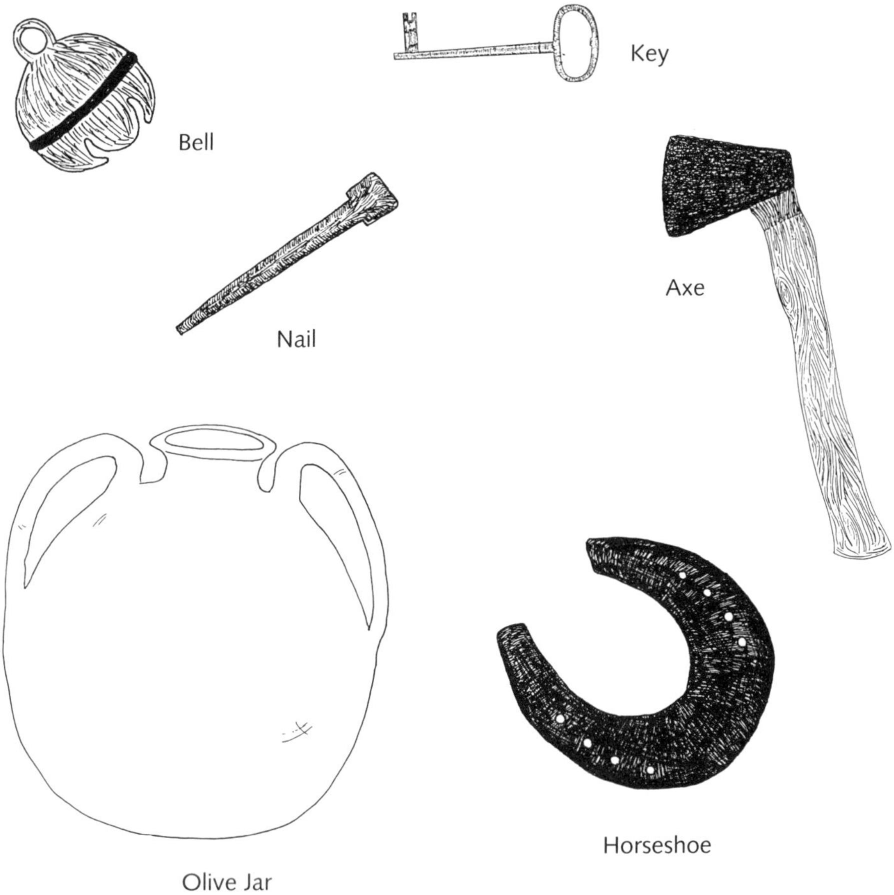

Fig. RR. Spanish tools

Because the soldiers, priests, officials, entrepreneurs, Africans, and native people all had different goals, there was plenty of conflict in early Florida. Read the next few chapters to discover how these conflicts affected Florida's native people.

40

Many Soldiers

Many soldiers came to Florida during the 1500s. The following list shows a few, along with the date each soldier arrived and the country that sent him.

Ponce de León (PON-se deh Leh-ON), 1513, from Spain

Pánfilo de Narváez (PAN-fee-low deh Nar-VAY-ez), 1528, from Spain

Hernando de Soto (Her-NAN-doe deh SO-toe), 1539, from Spain

Jean Ribault (Zhan REE-bow), 1562, from France

René de Laudonnière (Reh-NAY deh Law-don-ee-YER), 1564, from France

Pedro Menéndez (PE-drow Meh-NEN-dez), 1566, from Spain

What did these soldiers do in Florida? We know they worked to map Florida and make it safe for other Europeans. To accomplish this, they had to explore the coastline, the rivers, and the land. Exploring is hungry work, and most of the European soldiers ran out of food before they were finished. The Spanish solved this problem by taking food from the native people. They also forced some Indians to work as guides, interpreters, or equipment carriers.

Ponce de León and Pánfilo de Narváez fought battles with the native people during their visits. In some battles, they killed native people or took them as slaves. Other battles ended in trade. These early visits shaped the ways native people would think of Europeans.

Hernando de Soto marched an army of 500 Spanish soldiers through native lands, taking corn to feed his army along the way. As de Soto traveled, he killed hundreds of native people, including several chiefs. Stories about de Soto spread through native villages around Florida.

Other smaller expeditions followed, but the native people had learned from de Soto. If they heard the Spanish coming, they burned their own fields and huts and fled into the forest. When the Spanish arrived, there was no food to steal and no one to kidnap.

Jean Ribault and René de Laudonnière also made an impression on the Timucua people. While building **Fort Caroline** not far from where Jacksonville is today, the French ran low on food. They traded with the Timucua to get more, but finally ran out of things to trade. When this happened, Laudonnière kidnapped Chief Outina and tried to trade him for food. Outina's people refused to make the trade because they no longer trusted the French. Eventually Outina was freed.

When the Spanish government heard the French were building a fort in Florida, they sent General Pedro Menéndez to destroy it. Each country wanted Florida for itself, so the French leader, Ribault, decided to attack the Spanish at St. Augustine. When he sailed south from Fort Caroline, his ships were wrecked by a tropical storm. (See figure SS.) Menéndez captured and killed almost all the French people. Only a few managed to escape, including Jacques le Moyne. Le Moyne was the artist who drew the original pictures of the Timucua. Later, Theodore de Bry engraved le Moyne's artwork. You can see examples of these engravings in figures J, L, P, W, X, SS, WW, and ZZ on pages 38, 41, 49, 76, 178, 189, and 203.

After this battle, Menéndez continued to explore Florida. He also invited **Jesuit** priests to come to the New World and teach Florida's native people about Christianity. One priest, named Father Rogel (Ro-HEL), worked with the Calusa. Many conflicts arose among the Calusa people, the priests, and the Spanish soldiers. Chief Calos began looking for ways to make the Spanish priests and soldiers leave. These Europeans finally did leave, but not before killing two chiefs, including Calos. Soldiers caused great upheaval in the lives of Florida's native people. But the biggest changes were yet to come.

Fig. SS. French engraving of Jean Ribault's ships, by Theodore de Bry

41

A Changing Way of Life

European priests had a huge impact on Florida's native people. In 1578, **Franciscan** priests arrived in the New World to teach Florida's Indians about Christianity. (See figure TT.) The native people had become wary of all Europeans and were reluctant to welcome the Franciscans. These priests became even more unpopular when they tried to persuade the Indians to give up many of their beliefs and traditions. To get the native people to listen to their sermons, the Franciscans gave them corn, clothing, and tools.

In time, the priests set up **mission** churches throughout Timucua and Apalachee territories. By 1655, there were 38 missions in Florida. One of the mission priests was Father Francisco Pareja (Fran-SIS-ko Pa-REH-ha). Pareja wrote the *Confessionario*, our main source of information about the Timucua language.

In less than 100 years, most of the Timucua and Apalachee people stopped living in their traditional ways. Instead, they lived at mission villages like Spanish Christians. Priests also tried to set up a mission in Calusa territory, but the Calusa refused to become Christians and forced the priests to leave.

Why did the Timucua and Apalachee decide to change their ways of life? We can't be sure, but we can make some educated

Fig. TT. Franciscan priest

guesses. For example, we know that thousands of native people were dying from diseases like smallpox, measles, chickenpox, scarlet fever, typhus, malaria, bubonic plague, influenza, diphtheria, and yellow fever. Some historians think that European diseases killed almost nine out of every ten Florida Indians.

The native people didn't realize that the Europeans had introduced these germs to Florida. They just knew that their own traditional medicines, prayers, and healing chants could not stop the **epidemics** that swept through their villages. The Timucua and Apalachee may have felt that their traditional beliefs weren't working any more. Accepting Christian ideas may have been an attempt to keep their families safe and healthy.

Spanish technology also made Christianity attractive to the native people. Indians who became Christians received clothing, metal tools, and new kinds of seeds. The priests also taught the native people to read and write in Spanish and in Timucua. In exchange for this technology, the priests required native people make changes to their way of life, including cutting their hair, changing their names, and putting an end to the ball game.

Many native people who accepted these changes decided to move their villages close to a mission. Living at a mission meant obeying Spanish laws. One law said that native men had to work in St. Augustine for part of each year. As these men traveled back and forth between the missions and St. Augustine, they sometimes spread germs. As more and more native people died from European diseases, villages started to shrink. There weren't enough people left to plant their crops and still meet Spanish labor demands. Finally, the Timucua decided to revolt. The Timucua rebellion of 1656 did not last long. The Timucua killed a few Spanish soldiers and ranchers, but no priests. They just moved away from the missions. To punish the Timucua, Spanish soldiers killed several Timucua chiefs. The rebellion ended shortly after.

The Spanish government decided to move most Timucua villages to the Camino Real (Ka-ME-no Reh-AL), the main trail that connected St. Augustine to the Apalachee territory. (See figure UU.) The Spanish required that Timucua people keep this roadway clear and take travelers across the rivers. Many of these travelers also spread germs as they passed through.

Timucua people continued to die from disease, leaving fewer people in each village. Some villages joined together to increase their numbers. By 1675, there were only 11 missions with villages, instead of the 38 there had once been.

At the missions, Timucua and Apalachee people grew crops to feed themselves, the priests, and the people in St. Augustine. They grew corn and beans as they always had, but they also started to grow European crops, including watermelon, peaches, wheat, figs, hazelnuts, and oranges. They learned to raise chickens, pigs, cows, and horses.

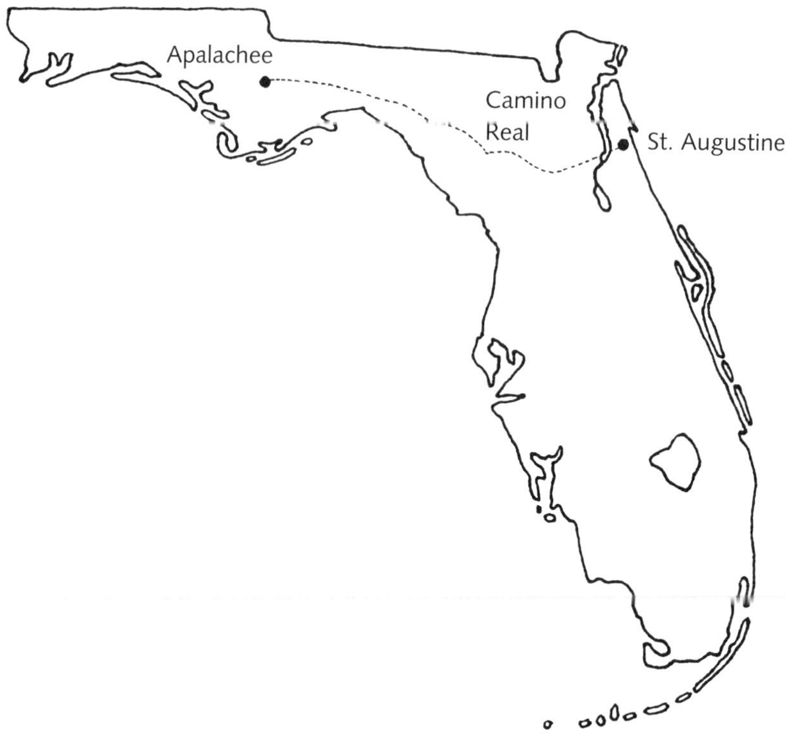

Fig. UU. Map of the Camino Real, from St. Augustine to Apalachee

While much of St. Augustine's food came from the missions, some came from Spanish farms and ranches. Spanish cattle ranchers were supposed to ask permission before building ranches on native lands. Each ranch had to be located far from the village cornfields, so the livestock would not eat the crops. Rules also defined the rights of native workers at Spanish ranches. However, some Spaniards paid no attention to these rules. In Apalachee territory, chiefs complained that Spanish cows were damaging their gardens. Sometimes native people who worked at the ranches did not get paid and were not allowed to go to church.

After the Timucua villages were rearranged along the Camino Real, the Spanish government gave the unused Timucua lands to Spanish farmers and ranchers. Eventually, there were 25 Spanish ranches in the Timucua territory—and only 11 Timucua villages.

42

An End and a Beginning

While the Spanish were busy in Florida, the English were setting up colonies to the north, on the coasts of Georgia, Virginia, and the Carolinas. The Spanish and English did not get along. In fact, the English were planning to push the Spanish out of North America. The Spanish knew this, and they tried to get ready for an attack. They required native men from Timucua and Apalachee mission villages to help build a stone fort at St. Augustine. This fort, Castillo de San Marcos, is still standing today.

Instead of attacking the Spanish stronghold in St. Augustine, the English worked to destroy the town's food sources. They convinced **Yamassee** Indians from Georgia to attack Spanish missions and ranches. Since the Yamassee had English guns, they won many battles. Thousands of Florida's native men, women, and children were taken north to English territory and sold as slaves. According to the Spanish governor, more than 12,000 native people were enslaved. The Yamassee also attacked the Camino Real. If food could not travel this road from Apalachee to St. Augustine, the Spanish would starve. Yamassee raids destroyed the ranches too, which meant no wheat or beef for St. Augustine. Spanish soldiers tried to protect the ranches and missions, but there were not enough soldiers to defend them all. The constant raids destroyed the missions and pushed most of Florida's remaining native people down to the southern part of the state. Only a few hundred Indians stayed near St. Augustine. By 1711, English raids had reached the southern tip of Florida. Many native people asked the Spanish to take them to Cuba, where they would be safe from the English.

By 1715, English slavers were also capturing many Yamassee, Guale, and Creek people in Georgia and Alabama. These native people moved close to St. Augustine, hoping for Spanish protection. However, the fort could barely protect itself and the two remaining mission villages. Spain was losing the war in Florida.

In 1763, Spain signed a treaty that gave Florida to the English. All of the Spanish people had to leave Florida or be ruled by England. Almost every Spaniard decided to leave. The 89 Indians living near St. Augustine chose to go to Cuba with them. As far as we know, there are no Timucua people left anywhere today.

While a few native people from south Florida villages might have survived, their cultures disappeared. They may have gone to Cuba by canoe, lived with Spanish fishermen, or blended in with the **Seminole** who came to south Florida. As far as we know, there are no more Calusa people.

Several Apalachee families survived these hardships. After the missions were destroyed, they escaped to the west and settled in Louisiana. Today, Apalachee people still live there. The Apalachee chief is named Gilmer Bennet.

Who are the Seminole? Creek Indians from Alabama and Georgia moved into Florida to escape the English slavers. By 1750, the first Creek villages were forming in Florida. Any Timucua, Apalachee, or Calusa people who stayed in Florida probably joined these villages for protection. The first Creek towns were located far from St. Augustine. Because these native people lived so far from the cities and missions, the Spanish called them *cimarrón*, a Spanish word that means "wild" or "untamed." The name came to be pronounced "Seminole" over time. There may have been as many as 5,000 Seminole people living in Florida then. They settled in areas where the Timucua and Apalachee once lived building open-air thatched huts called **chickees**. (See figure VV.)

When Florida became a territory of the United States in 1819, many settlers moved in from northern states and caused conflicts with the Seminole people. The Treaty of Moultrie Creek in 1823 tried to solve these conflicts. It moved all the Seminole people to areas south of Ocala. As time passed, the settlers kept coming. They wanted the Seminole lands south of Ocala too.

Fig. VV. Seminole chickee hut

When the Second Seminole War ended in 1842, the U.S. government forced most of the Seminoles to move to Oklahoma. About 250 Seminole people were able to hide and survive in the swamps of the Florida Everglades.

Just a few years later, in 1845, Florida became a state. More settlers moved in, and they wanted to use all of Florida's lands. Two hundred more Seminole people were captured and moved far away. The few Seminole people who escaped hid deep in the Everglades. They are the great-grandmothers and great-grandfathers of the Seminole people who live in Florida today.

The Seminole today are made up of two native groups who speak different languages. One group is called Seminole, and they speak Muskogee. The other group is called Miccosukee, and they speak the Mikasuki language. (Mikasuki is very much like the language the Apalachee once spoke.)

In the year 2000, there were 53,561 Native Americans living in Florida, representing 48 different native groups. Most of these people are Cherokees, but many Miccosukees, Seminoles, Poarch Creeks, Lumbee, Choctaw, Chippewa, and other native cultures are part of Florida today.

To learn more about Florida's modern native people, you can check out books and websites, visit native gatherings, or simply talk to native people you meet at school, in stores, or anyplace else. Look at the section in this book called "Native American Places to Visit" to find out where you can learn more.

In the next chapter, you'll go back to 1562, before the Spanish missions spread across Florida and before the English began raiding and taking slaves. To find out what might have happened when the Timucua met the first French soldiers, keep on reading.

43

Strangers

New characters in this section:

Maweeha (Ma-WEE-ha): A twelve-year-old Timucua girl

Ribault (Ree-BOW): The leader of a French expedition to Florida

Pierre (Pee-AIR): A sailor on the French expedition

Tenerife chewed a handful of garlic bulbs in the hot morning sun. It was their first morning at the fishing camp, and tiny gnats were swarming them. Tenerife bit into another garlic bulb, wishing the strong smell would begin to repel the gnats right away.

"These gnats are terrible!" Emisu shouted. He and the older children slapped at their arms and legs. Only the two youngest sat quietly. They were busy building huts with the marsh mud. The gnats weren't bothering them at all.

Tenerife was about to tell the others to smear on some mud when he heard "Mud fight!"

Tenerife watched the first handful of mud slide down Simaru's chest. The boy whipped around and lobbed a double handful at Emisu. Maweeha ran to the water's edge and scooped up a basketful of mud, then emptied the whole thing over Kidawe's head. While little Leena was laughing, Kidawe grabbed a handful of their mud hut and rubbed it in her hair.

"You're prettier with the mud on!" he said.

"Then you must be beautiful, brother!" Emisu laughed, and Kidawe scrambled to his feet and took off after him. Simaru tackled them both and sent them tumbling into the deeper water. A cool breeze blew in from the salt marsh, carrying the biting gnats away from them all.

"Anacotima!" Emisu shouted. "It's two against one. Help me!"

"Rally the girls," Tenerife called back. "They can save you. Maweeha!" he called. "Leena! Emisu needs your help!"

"I do not!" Emisu shouted.

The girls jumped into the jumble of arms and legs and dunked Emisu under the water.

Tenerife grinned and looked back down at the stone knife blade he was making. He had lived through a full cycle of moons since people had started calling him "Anacotima" again. Emisu had completed his first adult hunt, and Tenerife had watched the boy grow nearly a footstep in height. All the children were changing, even little Leena.

"Got you!" Leena was clinging to Emisu's back, with her fingers twined tightly through his long black hair.

"Okay, I give!" Emisu shouted. "Four to one isn't fair."

"So what!" Leena said. "You should have asked the girls to help!" Leena slid off Emisu's back and splashed into the water. "Let's wash this mud off!" she said and dunked her muddy hair beneath the surface. Simaru and Kidawe splashed into the deeper marsh water, and Emisu dove in behind them. Maweeha rinsed the mud from her hair and glanced up at the horizon.

Tenerife watched her smile fade.

"Look!" Maweeha pointed to the horizon.

Saltbrush bushes blocked Tenerife's view, so he waded out into

Fig. WW. French engraving of Jean Ribault and his men approaching the Timucua, by Theodore de Bry

the hip-deep water. He saw a boat sailing toward them—twice as wide as a canoe and twice as long. While he watched, another boat came over the horizon, then another.

Emisu gripped Maweeha's hand and sloshed toward Tenerife. "Who are they?"

Tenerife didn't answer. He just stared at the boats, lost in a memory from long ago.

"Anacotima," Emisu said. "What should we do?"

44

Face to Face

"Back to shore! Now!" Tenerife grabbed the younger children's hands and pulled them along. His leg ached from his old injury as he struggled toward shore. He could hear the older children pushing through the muddy water behind him. Memories of the Spanish flashed through his mind. Had they finally come for him?

When they made it to shore, Tenerife stood breathing heavily, with his hands resting on his knees. Pain spiked through his right leg, but he ignored it and focused on the boats. They seemed much closer than before. Each one had more than ten people in it. Tenerife felt all the children staring at him, waiting.

"Anacotima, what do we do?" Emisu asked. "They're too close for us to run. We could never make it back to the fishing camp."

"Is it Outina's warriors?" Maweeha asked.

"No, children. They have no boats like that. I think it's the Spanish."

"The Spanish!" Emisu said. "But they've never come here! Why would they come?"

"For me, maybe," Tenerife said.

"Will they shoot us, Anacotima?" Kidawe asked.

"I don't think so. Leena, Kidawe, quickly, go hide in the

saltbrush. Watch to see what happens. Then run to camp and tell the others." Kidawe and Leena looked at each other, still breathing hard. "No more fighting," Tenerife said. "You have to protect each other." Tenerife watched them vanish into the saltbrush.

"What about us, Anacotima?" Maweeha asked.

"Whoever is coming in those boats might kidnap a lone man. But together, we may be safe. Boys," Tenerife put his hands on their shoulders, "if anything happens to me, I am counting on you to protect Maweeha. Don't let them take her." They nodded.

Tenerife gripped his half-made knife and stood as straight as his bad leg would hold him. If only Sheko were here.... More than twenty men splashed into the shallow water and dragged the large canoes onto the marsh mud. Tenerife breathed in deeply. He would not let them take these children!

"Do not speak," Tenerife whispered. "I will not let them know I understand the Spanish words. Perhaps they will leave."

Tenerife watched quietly as the strangers approached. Most of them were no taller than Emisu, well under six footsteps tall. Their faces were hairy, and their skin looked pale and sickly. Their clothes hung on their arms, fitting poorly. These were not the clothes of priests. These colorful garments were the mark of warriors.

Tenerife thought quickly. If he spoke first, he would look stronger in the strangers' eyes. He walked along the line of soldiers, inspecting them for strengths and weaknesses.

One of the men was leaning on another. His face was flushed pink. Tenerife spoke to the children. "This man is ill. Simaru, please lay him down on the pine straw mat. Be careful of his skin. He has sores on his face. Do not touch them. Many of the dark skins died of a sickness like this. Our shaman might know how to heal him."

Simaru motioned to the sick man, leading him away from the spot where Leena and Kidawe hid. He laid the stranger down on the pine needles and stood guard over him.

Tenerife nodded. Having a prisoner might help them to bargain, if it came to that. He continued walking in front of the strangers, trying to look tall and regal, like a chief. He couldn't tell which of the strangers was the leader. They all stood together, as though equals. Tenerife spoke a silent plea to Father Sun. "Help me make the right choice," he thought. "Help me save these children."

Then he saw it. A sign. One of the strangers had hair the color of Father Sun. The man looked young, not much older than Emisu. But if Father Sun had marked him, he had to be honorable.

Tenerife spoke in his own language to the sun-colored man. He would give no hint that he could speak the Spanish words. "Who are you?" he said. "Are you friends of the Saturiwa?"

The sun-colored man bit his bottom lip and walked over to another of the strangers. This one had dark hair and a shiny helmet. Perhaps the helmet was a sign of favor from their leader. The sun-colored man pointed to him and said "Ribault."

Tenerife repeated "Ree-bow." The sun-colored man smiled and nodded. Tenerife didn't dare tell them his own name. What if they really had come for him? Instead, he pointed at Emisu and raised his hand up to show how tall their chief was. "Saturiwa."

Ribault spoke the name slowly. "Sa-cher-ee-wuh." Tenerife nodded. What could he do to make the soldiers go away?

Just then, the boys' fathers crashed through the saltbrush behind them. The strangers pulled out **arquebusses** and long shiny knives.

"No!" Tenerife stepped between the strangers and his people. He held his arms up, spread wide. Both groups backed away. The long knives disappeared into the strangers' clothes, but the

Fig. XX. French soldier

arquebusses did not. The fathers lowered their bows but didn't put them down.

Tenerife signaled Emisu to tell his father about the strangers, never taking his eyes off their weapons. He watched a soldier shift his arquebus. Were they going to attack?

Tenerife heard the fathers walk up to stand at his side. "Anacotima," they whispered. "Are they Spanish?"

"I believe they are, but I haven't heard them speak much. They do not know my name. Let us keep it that way. I haven't spoken the Spanish words either. I don't wish to spend the rest of my life as a Spanish slave."

The fathers nodded. "The children are building a fire to make willow-bark tea for the sick one. Let us sit and talk with their leader. His name?" they asked.

"Ree-bow."

Tenerife gestured for Ribault to follow him to the fire. Ribault and one of his soldiers sat to the east, away from the heat of the fire. They slapped furiously at gnats, and Tenerife tried not to grin. He and the fathers sat to the west of the fire, letting its hot smoke cover them and push the bugs away. The fathers were having a hard time not laughing as well. These strangers didn't know anything about the way the world worked. Who avoided smoke on a buggy day?

Tenerife called to Maweeha. "Bring us some water, please. And get the boys to help you gather oysters. These men need food."

She nodded and ran to get a bladder of water. The men sat together, sharing the food and drink provided by the children. Ribault spoke a few sentences and waited.

"I don't know what he is saying," Tenerife whispered to the fathers. "It's been so long. Maybe I've forgotten."

Through gestures, Tenerife and the fathers told Ribault to come back the next morning. They could meet with Chief Saturiwa then. It took a while to get their message across, but Ribault finally nodded.

Tenerife watched as the strangers climbed back into their boats. Why hadn't he been able to understand their words? They looked and acted like Spanish soldiers. Could he have forgotten their language? He walked over and looked down at the sick man. They had left him sleeping on the pine-straw mat. "Maweeha," Tenerife called. "Care for this man. Don't let him die. But do not stay close to him. His illness is catching." He watched her feed the stranger sips of willow-bark tea, then looked back at the marsh.

As the strangers' boats disappeared over the horizon, the fathers called to Leena and Kidawe. "Come out of hiding, children."

Leena and Kidawe jogged over to the fire and hugged their fathers. "How did you know to come?" Kidawe asked them.

"We saw their ships while we were seal hunting. We came as fast as we could."

"Where is mother?" Leena asked.

"The women stayed at the fishing camp in case you returned." Emisu's father turned to the older man. "Anacotima, we are grateful to you for protecting our children."

Tenerife nodded. "We must get word to the chief. I think the men should stay, in case the strangers return in the night." When the fathers nodded, Tenerife looked at the older boys. "Emisu and Simaru, canoe back to the village. Bring the chief, the shaman, and Sheko."

"We'll go like the wind, Anacotima. We know the way."

Tenerife nodded. "Good, then go. There's no time to spare."

"I could go too, Anacotima," Kidawe said. "I'm big enough."

Tenerife smiled. "Yes, you are. But we need you here, Kidawe, to help watch for the strangers' return. Can you do this?"

Kidawe took a deep breath and stood up straighter. "Yes, Anacotima. I can protect our camp."

"Girls," Tenerife said, "we must move the fishing camp to this spot. The women and men will need your help. Will you do this?"

"Yes," Maweeha said. "And we'll take care of the sick man."

"Only you, Maweeha. Leena must stay away from him. Go now; help Emisu and Simaru prepare for their journey."

Tenerife watched the children jog off, looking excited and serious about their tasks. Then he turned to the fathers. "What weapons do we have? In case the strangers return in the night."

Emisu's father gripped Tenerife's shoulder. "Don't worry, Anacotima. We will be ready."

"Do you think we can make a treaty with them?" Simaru's father asked. "I'd like one of those long metal knives."

"They might make a treaty," Tenerife said. "But I don't know if they would honor it. I've heard stories of broken treaties from many villages to the south and west. If Chief Saturiwa does want a treaty, he should ask for arquebusses. They hold the real power. With those, we could defeat Outina in every battle." Tenerife stood slowly, feeling the ache in his leg creep up into his back. "Let's get back to camp." He spoke loud enough for the children to hear. "There is much to be done before the strangers return." Tenerife watched the horizon for any sign of boats or ships. As he walked, he had a sudden memory of being tied and dragged through the forest. It would be a long night.

45

Friends or Enemies?

The next morning Tenerife awoke long before Father Sun. He watched as three canoes approached. Emisu and Simaru paddled the front canoe, leading the way for Chief Saturiwa, the shaman, and their closest advisors. Tenerife looked to see if a fourth canoe was coming up behind them, but none followed. Sheko must have been away on the hunt. Tenerife frowned. He would have to do this alone. Far away, on the horizon, three small specks appeared. The strangers were coming.

Tenerife sat with Chief Saturiwa in the shade of the **paha.** The chief was putting on Ashefa's silver ear spools. Tenerife grinned. It had probably been Ashefa's idea. The jewelry would help make a strong impression on the strangers.

The chief also wore a painted loincloth. Tattoos dotted his skin, and shell beads decorated his arms and legs. A long red egret feather topped his hair knot. The women had set up a feast around him: platters of seasoned corn mush, cattail shoots, dried fruit, seal steaks, oyster stew, and broiled fish.

Everyone stood motionless as the strangers dragged their boats onshore. Ribault of the Shining Helmet walked over and stood before Saturiwa. When the chief refused to stand, Ribault sat down as well. They both spoke, but neither understood the other's words.

Fig. YY. Chief Saturiwa

Tenerife listened closely to the stranger's rolling voice. It sounded like Spanish, but he couldn't understand it. When Ribault stopped speaking, the chief tapped Tenerife on the arm.

Tenerife swallowed hard. He had told the chief over and over that he couldn't understand the strangers' words. But the chief was firm. Tenerife knew more about these strangers than anyone there. He must try to make a treaty.

Tenerife took a deep breath, trying out the words silently in his head before he spoke them. "Como está usted?" he finally said.

"Me llamo Anacotima. Deseamos amistad." ["How are you? I am Anacotima. We want friendship."] He smiled hopefully at the strangers.

But Ribault did not smile back. He shouted angry words and pulled out a long knife. The other strangers ran to his side.

In a flash, Emisu leaped in front of Tenerife. "No!" he shouted. "Fight a young man if you have to!" Emisu held the half-finished stone knife close to Ribault's throat.

Tenerife turned to Saturiwa. The chief said nothing. He looked perfectly calm and in control.

Ribault was watching the chief's reaction too. Slowly, he set down his weapon. The other strangers set theirs down as well, and the chief gestured for Emisu to sit beside him.

Ribault sat down slowly and spoke to Tenerife, this time in Spanish. "I am sorry. The words you used are the words of our enemies, the Spanish. We are French. Are the men who taught you these Spanish words still here?"

Tenerife shook his head. He stared into the air next to Ribault, trying to remember the words from long ago. Finally, he spoke. "The Spanish are enemies to us. They steal people."

Ribault nodded. "The French want friendship. No stealing."

Chief Saturiwa whispered to Emisu. The boy picked up a deer hide. It was painted with pictures of all the animals the people hunted. The chief also handed Emisu the bright red egret feather from his hair.

Tenerife turned to Ribault and said, "Gifts of friendship," as Emisu set the deer hide and egret feather near Ribault's crossed legs. Tenerife watched the French leader. Would Ribault honor Saturiwa's gifts by sharing some of his own?

Ribault whispered to the sun-colored stranger, and the man

brought gifts to Saturiwa. These gifts were strange metal things. One was two knives joined in the middle. It had holes that fit a finger and thumb, so the knives could be squeezed shut. Ribault showed how easy it was to cut a piece of palm rope between those joined knives. He also gave Saturiwa a bracelet of shining metal.

The chief showed Ribault three metal pieces he had won in battle from Outina. When Ribault reached for them, the chief pulled them back.

"Is that silver?" Ribault asked. Tenerife shook his head to show he didn't know that word.

Ribault pointed to the silver shapes again, then to Ashefa's ear spools. "Donde?"

Tenerife turned to whisper to the chief. "He wants to know where we got this metal. Should I tell him?"

The chief nodded.

Tenerife turned back to Ribault. "We captured it from Thimagona," he said, gesturing to the southwest.

Ribault repeated the word slowly. "Tee-mo-go-na."

Tenerife listened as the word for "enemy" rolled off the stranger's tongue. He shifted uncomfortably. Was it an omen that Ribault's first word was "enemy"?

Chief Saturiwa tapped Tenerife's arm. "Come, Anacotima. Let them sit and wait awhile. Decisions must be made."

46

New Treaties

The advisors and the shaman followed Chief Saturiwa to another paha, where the strangers couldn't watch. "We should ask for weapons," the chief said. "What do you say?"

Tenerife spoke up. "I don't think they will give them to us. They don't trust us."

Chief Saturiwa nodded. "So we are to expect problems. Knowing this makes us wiser. But I still wish to pursue a treaty."

Another advisor spoke. "If we ask for nothing, they won't respect us. They will see us as a small brother to be ordered around. We must show our strength."

"I have an idea," Tenerife said. "We could tell them that we are impressed with their weapons, and that the next time we meet, they must give us five long knives and five arquebusses. We are showing we have the right to ask. But it won't force them to say no."

The chief agreed. "This is a good idea. But what should we ask for now?"

Several of the advisors made suggestions: some of the strangers' clothing, more metal tools, Ribault's helmet.

"Yes, yes," the chief said. "These are all good things, but they are things a small brother would beg for. What can we demand? What will make them respect us?"

"The sun-colored man!" Tenerife said. "Make them give us the sun-colored man. He'll bring luck to our village. Ribault will see that we understand the value of things. He will respect us."

"Yes," one of the advisors said. "Ask for the smaller things, but demand the sun-colored man."

The chief nodded. "This is the way. And offer them all of the food and water laid out here. They look half-starved. Come, Anacotima; use your skills once more to tell Ribault our decision."

Tenerife walked back to the soldiers, who were talking their French talk in quick flowing bursts. He motioned Ribault forward and told him all that the chief had ordered.

"Yes," Ribault said. "Next time we come, we will bring you many weapons. Your chief is wise to ask." He took off his own helmet and handed it to Tenerife. "Give this to your chief." Ribault turned to call to one of his men. "Pierre!" The sun-colored man walked over. Ribault told him to gather clothing and tools for the chief. The sun-colored man walked back to their boats and rummaged through a wooden box.

Tenerife paused. He felt sure that Ribault hadn't told the sun-colored man to stay. "We must have the sun-colored man," Tenerife said in a strong voice. "We must."

Ribault nodded. "And we are to have all of the food and water here?"

"Yes." Tenerife called to the women to package the food for travel. They worked quickly. By the time the sun-colored man returned, other soldiers were loading food into the boats.

Tenerife spoke loudly. "Ribault and his people are friends of our friends. They will go back to their boat now. But they will give us many gifts, and the sun-colored man will stay to bring us luck."

Tenerife watched the sun-colored man. He still didn't realize he was to stay. Ribault summoned the sun-colored man and spoke to him quietly. Tenerife couldn't understand their words, but he knew the sun-colored man was upset.

The strange men argued, but finally, the sun-colored man turned away from his leader and his people. He took a deep breath and sat down by the fire.

Ribault shouted to his men. They finished loading the boats and pushed off. Tenerife and the others watched the boats until they disappeared over the horizon. The small children, quiet and still for so long, were suddenly noisy. Kidawe poked Leena with a piece of sharp needlerush grass, then took off running. Leena leaped into a sprint, chasing after him. Tenerife heard several people laugh. It had been a tense morning. A little laughter would do them all good.

Fig. ZZ. French engraving of friendship between the Timucua and the French, by Theodore de Bry

The shaman stood and stretched his legs. "Where is this sick man?" he asked. "I should tend to him."

"I can show you," Maweeha said.

Maweeha's mother was working to calm the sun-colored man. He sat quietly now but looked terribly frightened. "Perhaps I should try to explain," Tenerife thought. "He's not a slave; he's an honored guest. Maybe he speaks the Spanish words." As Tenerife reassured the sun-colored man, the chief called to him.

"Anacotima," he said. "This is a day to be remembered in story! Come! Tell us the tale."

Everyone gathered in the shade of the pahas, sipping mint tea and whispering. Cicadas buzzed in the hot air. A sudden breeze cooled them, and Tenerife began his tale. "This is a time of change," he said. "A time of new treaties and brave futures. Let me tell you how it started."

Native American Places to Visit

The phone numbers and websites listed below are accurate as of summer 2002. If you have problems reaching these sites, you can call information for phone assistance or search the internet by typing in the name of the site.

Panhandle Area

Lake Jackson Mounds.

Hike over mounds made by ancestors of the Apalachee.

3600 Indian Mound Road
Tallahassee, FL 32303
(850) 922-6007
http://www.dep.state.fl.us/parks/district1/lakejackson/

Museum of Florida History.

Enjoy the murals of Archaic and Paleo-Indians and see plenty of artifacts.

500 South Bronough Street
Tallahassee, FL 32399-0250
(850) 488-1484
http://dhr.dos.state.fl.us/museum

San Luis Archaeological Site.

Explore the council house and touch re-created native pots, tools, and animal furs.

2020 West Mission Road
Tallahassee, FL 32034
(850) 487-3711
http://dhr.dos.state.fl.us/dhr/bar/san_luis/

Northeast Florida

Castillo de San Marcos.

Explore the Spanish fort in St. Augustine, built in the 1600s.

1 South Castillo Drive
St. Augustine, FL 32084
(904) 829-6506
http://www.nps.gov/casa

Florida Museum of Natural History.

Explore the Calusa way of life through models of thatched huts, mangrove swamps, and computer graphics.

Powell Hall
S.W. 34th Street and Hull Road
Box 112710, University of Florida
Gainesville, FL 32611-2710
(352) 846-2000, ext. 212
http://www.flmnh.ufl.edu

Ft. Caroline National Memorial.

Walk nature trails and look at museum exhibits on the Timucua and the French. See replicas of the French Fort Caroline and the Jean Ribault monument.

12713 Ft. Caroline Road
Jacksonville, FL 32225
(904) 641-7155
http://www.nps.gov/foca

Heritage of the Ancient Ones.

Explore a re-created native village and attend workshops on native toolmaking and pottery making.

4202 24th Street S.E.
Ruskin, FL 33570
Phone for reservations: (813) 641-8545
http://www.ancientnative.org

Jacksonville Museum of Science and History.

Visit the "Currents of Time" exhibit to see Timucua artifacts and learn about the Spanish and French in Florida.

1025 Museum Circle
Jacksonville, FL 32207
(904) 396-7062
http://www.themosh.org

Morningside Nature Center.

Hike nature trails and try native gardening, music making, and rope weaving.

3540 E. University Avenue
Gainesville, FL 32641
(352) 334-2170
http://www.natureoperations.org/NP&Fframes.htm

Museum of Arts and Sciences at Daytona Beach.

Check out the skeleton of a 12-foot-tall prehistoric sloth to see an animal the Paleo-Indians hunted. See native tools and jewelry, a model of a burial mound, two copies of totem poles, and a touch-screen history computer.

1040 Museum Blvd.
Daytona Beach, FL 32114
(386) 255-0285
http://www.moas.org

Paynes Prairie State Preserve.

Check out the visitor's center and native displays.

100 Savannah Blvd. (off U.S. 441 south of Gainesville)
Micanopy, FL 32667
(352) 466-3397
http://www.afn.org/~pprairie/

Pelotes Island Nature Preserve.

Classes, scouts, and other groups can make reservations to hike over middens, see a native hut, and try native skills and games.

11201 New Berlin Road
Jacksonville, FL 32226
(904) 665-8856
http://pelotes.jea.com

Silver River Museum.

Check out a mammoth skeleton, a prehistoric shark jaw, and plenty of native projectile points.

1445 N.E. 58th Avenue
Ocala, FL 34470
(352) 236-5401
http://www.dialplus.net/srm

Talbot Island State Parks.

Hike over shell middens shaped like giant rings.

12157 Heckscher Drive
Jacksonville, FL 32226
(904) 251-2320
http://www.floridastateparks/district2/bigtalbot/index.asp

Theodore Roosevelt Area of the Timucua Preserve.

Hike across 30 acres of middens in wild Florida.

12713 Ft. Caroline Road
Jacksonville, FL 32225
(904) 221-5568
http://www.nps.gov/timu/index.htm

Tomoka River State Park.

Hike trails and check out projectile points and modern paintings of the Timucua.

2099 North Beach Street
Ormond Beach, FL 32174
(386) 676-4050
http://www.floridastateparks/district3/tomoka/index.asp

Central Florida

Brevard Museum of History and Natural Sciences.

Explore a hands-on fossil exhibit and 22 acres of nature trails. Mannequins show Seminole people and the 7,000-year-old Windover archaeological site.

2201 Michigan Avenue
Cocoa, FL 32926
(321) 632-1830
http://www.brevardmuseum.com

Canaveral National Seashore.

Hike over huge middens and check out native tools.

7611 South Atlantic Avenue (Highway A1A)
New Smyrna Beach, FL 32169
(386) 427-6126
http://www.nps.gov/cana/index.htm

Crystal River State Archaeological Site.

Hike native mounds and explore museum displays on archaeology and native history.

3400 North Museum Point
Crystal River, FL 34428
(352) 795-3817
http://www.citruscounty-fl.com/CrysRiv.html

Ft. Christmas Historical Museum and Parks.

Explore a rebuilt 1837 Seminole War Fort and check out native artifacts.

1300 Ft. Christmas Road
Christmas, FL 32079
(407) 568-4149
http://www.nbbd.com/godo/FortChristmas/

Hontoon Island State Park.

Go hiking and biking on midden trails and see copies of owl and otter totem poles.

2309 River Ridge Road
Deland, FL 32720
(386) 736-5309
http://www.planetdeland.com/hontoon/

Madira Bickel Mound State Archaeological Site.

Hike to the top of the Madira Bickel Mound, a 20-foot-high ceremonial mound of shell and sand.

3708 Patten Avenue
Ellenton, FL 34222
(941) 723-4536

Orange County Historical Museum.

Check out a dugout canoe and other native artifacts.

812 East Rollins Street
Orlando, FL 32803
1-800-965-2030
http://www.thehistorycenter.org

Seminole County Student Museum.

Explore a museum set up as a Timucua village with a hut, a canoe, a meat-drying rack, and a mural on all four walls.

301 Seventh Street
Sanford, FL 32711-2505
(407) 320-0520
http://www.millenium.scps.k12.fl.us/smusem.html

South Florida Museum.

Check out native artifacts and murals of prehistoric animals.

201 10th Street West
West Bradenton, FL 34205
(941) 746-4131
http://www.southfloridamuseum.org

South Florida

Arch Creek Park.

Hike the Tequesta Nature Trail, including five acres of midden, and explore the museum's artifacts.

1855 N.E. 135th Street
North Miami, FL 33161
(305) 944-6111
http://www.co.miami-dade.fl.us/parks/Parks/arch_creek.htm

Calusa Nature Center and Planetarium.

Explore cypress swamps and native huts.

3450 Ortiz Avenue
Ft. Myers, FL 33905
(941) 275-3435
http://www.calusanature.com

Glossary

Amphibian: A cold-blooded animal that spends one part of its life breathing water with gills and another part breathing air with lungs—for example, a frog.

Archaeologist (ar-kee-AH-low-jist): A person who investigates the past by studying things that animals, plants, or people left behind.

Arquebus (AR-ke-bus): A heavy rifle-like gun invented in the 1400s. (See figure XX on page 193.)

Artifact: Any man-made object. Native artifacts include pottery, tools, artwork, and anything else native people made.

Ashes: The grayish-white material that remains after wood burns. Ash was used as an antiseptic to prevent infection and was also added to flour to help bread rise.

Atlatl (at-LAT-el): A hand-held hunting tool that launched short spears for great distances. They were used less after the invention of the bow and arrow.

Burial mound: A place where dead people are laid on the ground and covered with sand. As more bodies and sand are added, it creates a hill or mound. (See figure K on page 39.)

Canal: An artificial waterway or an improved ditch or stream.

Cane: A bamboo-like plant, also called river cane, used to make shafts for arrows, spears, and atlatl darts, as well as smooth benches and fish traps.

Cassina (kuh-SEE-na): A ceremonial drink made from the caffeinated leaves of a Yaupon holly plant. Its scientific name is *Ilex vomitoria.*

Ceremonial: Actions or art that describe or try to control the natural world through religion, power, or wealth.

Charnel house: A hut where the bodies of dead people were kept until only bones remained.

Check-stamped pottery: Coiled pottery decorated by pressing a wooden paddle onto a soft, unfinished pot. The paddle was carved with criss-cross designs that transferred criss-cross markings onto the clay. These markings became permanent when the pot was hardened in a fire. There were several types of check-stamp pottery, each with a different kind of criss-cross pattern.

Chert: White rock, usually found in central Florida limestone deposits, the main toolmaking rock found in Florida. "Flint" is a darker, higher-quality stone seldom found in Florida. "Flintknapping" is toolmaking with stone.

Chickee: A rectangular home used by historic Seminole people. A wooden floor was raised above the ground, walls were open to the air, and the roof was thatched with palm fronds. (See figure VV on page 185.)

Chiefdom: The many villages ruled by one head chief.

Clan: All of the people a native person thought of as relatives. Most Florida native groups were matrilineal, which means they traced their relatives through their mothers. If you visited another village, people in your clan would give you a place to sleep and treat you like family, even if you had never met before.

Cocci bug or **cochineal insect** (KO-chi-neel): Warm-weather insects found on prickly-pear cactuses in south Florida. When squashed, these insects make a deep reddish dye, which is used as food coloring in many of the red foods we eat today.

Coiled pottery: Light, thin bowls and other clay items made by rolling clay into long ropes, coiling them into a shape, smoothing away all of the lines, and then hardening the pot in a fire. (See figure Y on page 84.)

Colonists: The first people from a culture to settle in a faraway place.

Columbus, Christopher: An Italian navigator credited with discovering America in A.D. 1492.

Complicated-stamped pottery: Coiled pottery decorated by pressing a wooden paddle onto a soft, unfinished clay pot. The paddle was carved with swirling designs that transferred swirling patterns onto the clay. These markings became permanent when the pot was hardened in a fire. There were several types of complicated-stamp pottery, each with a different kind of swirling pattern.

Council house: A large hut, often the center of a village or group of villages, that provided space for work, play, and celebrations.

Dark-skins: A term used in this story to describe Africans brought to the New World to work as slaves.

Drying rack: A bench high above the ground where strips of meat or vegetables are dried by the sun or by a smoky fire. Drying foods prevented spoiling.

Dugout: A canoe made by hollowing out a pine or cypress log. (See figure GG on page 121.)

Ember: A small piece of wood that is barely burning.

Engraving: A picture made by first carving a design into a block of wood (or some other material). The block is dipped in ink, then pressed onto a sheet of paper, transferring the design to the paper. Engraving allows you to make many exact copies of a design, drawing, or text.

Entrails: The internal organs of animals, which native people used for many purposes. For example, they made canteens from stomachs and waterproof tube-like containers from intestines.

Entrepreneur (on-treh-preh-NUR): A person who risks his or her own money and resources in a business venture.

Epidemic: The sudden, rapid spread of a contagious disease to many people.

Fiber-tempered pottery: The earliest kind of pottery made in Florida. Spanish moss fibers were mixed into wet clay, and then a thick slab of the clay was shaped into a pot. When the pot was hardened in a fire, the Spanish moss burned away, leaving squiggly marks behind. This technique made very thick, heavy pottery.

Fire board: A board with a hole drilled through it used to start fires. A stick was placed in the hole and spun with a fire bow. When the stick and board rubbed together, they created heat and sparks. Some sparks fell through the hole onto a pile of flammable material, such as plant fluff. This burnable material, or tinder, would catch fire if someone blew on the sparks gently. (Look at figure V on page 75.)

Footstep: A way to measure short distances (instead of feet or meters). Native people probably measured longer distances by how many days it took to make the trip.

Fort Caroline: A triangular French fort once located somewhere near Jacksonville, Florida.

Franciscan: A Roman Catholic group founded in A.D. 1209.

Frond: A leaf from a palm tree or fern.

Gig: Fishing spears that often had two spikes, used to stab at nearby fish.

Glacier: A huge layer of ice that covers the land.

Gorget (GOR-jet): A piece of jewelry or protective armor that covers the throat or chest. (See figure DD on page 108.)

Guacara River: Called the Suwannee River today. A mission called San Juan was located nearby. The native people called this river "San Juanee," and later that became "Suwannee."

Hand of days: Five days.

Hearth: A central fire that provided light, heat, and cooking space.

Historian: A person who studies the past by reading old stories and documents.

Hominy: Dried cracked corn kernels that were boiled in water until they were soft and puffy.
Honoso (ho-NO-so): A Timucua word meaning deer.
Human sacrifice: A person killed or sacrificed as a gift to a god. The Calusa practiced human sacrifice but *not* cannibalism—they did *not* eat people.
Huque (hoo-KEH): The Timucua word for hurricane.
Jesuit: A Roman Catholic group founded in A.D. 1534.
Lacrosse: A team sport played with racquets, balls, and goals. A version is still played today, using long racquets to sling balls toward a goal.
Leather: Animal hide with the fur scraped off, used by Native people to make clothing, pots, and bowstrings.
Mammoth: Prehistoric elephant, now extinct.
Marrow: Soft mixture of blood and tissue found inside bones. Many native groups ate this nutritious material.
Marsh: Treeless wetlands filled with freshwater or saltwater.
Matchcoat: Wrap-around coat made of leather or waterproof feathers.
Megafauna (MEG-uh-FAWN-uh): Very large animals that lived over 10,000 years ago. These animals, including mammoths, giant sloths, and saber-toothed tigers, are now extinct.
Midden: Native trash piles usually made of shells, animal bones, and broken tools like pottery and stone points.
Migrate: To move from one area to another in search of resources like food or space to live.
Mired: Stuck.
Mission: A building where Christian religious services were offered to Florida Indians.
Moon: Twenty-eight days, a little less than a month. There are 13 moons in a year instead of 12. For example, the Blueberry Moon comes around June, when blueberry bushes are in fruit.
Mortar: Large wooden bowls used for grinding nuts, grains, fruits,

and vegetables. Native people pounded these foods with a club called a pestle.

New World: North and South America, continents that were new to the Europeans. The Old World includes Europe, Africa, and Asia.

Nita (nee-TA): An Apalachee word meaning bear.

Nomads: Groups of people who have no home base and travel from place to place in search of food and water.

Omen: A sign that something is about to happen. For example, a popping fire is a Timucua bad omen. It suggests that war is coming. Today a black cat is a bad omen, suggesting that bad luck is coming.

***Paha*:** A Timucua word meaning hut or house.

Paleo-Indian (PAY-lee-oh): The first people to live in Florida, arriving 12,000 years ago.

Paramount chief: Chief with the highest authority and power, who ruled over many head chiefs.

Pass water: Urinate.

Potano: A group of people who lived near Gainesville. (See figure T on page 68.)

Poultice: A mixture of plant medicines with clay or dough, applied to the skin to treat surface injuries or muscle aches.

Purified: Made clean by removing all faults or weaknesses.

Sacerdote: The Spanish word for "priest."

Scalp: Skin that connects hair to the head.

Scandinavia: A peninsula of Northern Europe occupied by Norway and Sweden.

Scat: Dung, an animal's solid waste material.

Shaft: The long narrow part of an arrow or spear.

Shaman: A doctor or priest for native people.

Shellfish: Water animals that have shells, such as oysters, whelks, conches, mussels, and clams.

Sinew: Animal **tendon** that could be made into cord or thread.

Sinkhole: Natural hole in the ground that connects with an underground passage, often filled with water.
Sky spill: A sudden heavy downburst of rain and hail during a storm, which can cause as much damage as a tornado.
Slab pottery: Thick bowls and other clay items shaped from a rolled-out layer of clay. This heavy pottery was invented by Archaic Indians.
Slavers: Europeans who captured African Americans or Native Americans and sold them as slaves.
Smudge: A smoky fire used to protect crops or people from frost and insects.
Snare: A trap to catch small birds and mammals.
Solstice: The time of year when the sun is farthest from the earth. Each year, the summer solstice occurs around June 22 and the winter solstice about December 22.
Status: How important a person is in his or her community.
Tendon: Stringy connector that attaches muscle to bone.
Thatched roofs: Roofs made from weaving together thick layers of plant materials, like palm fronds.
Tide: Rise and fall of the ocean that brings water higher on shore (high tide) and farther away from the shore (low tide). In northeast Florida, high tide and low tide occur twice each day.
Tocobaga River (Toe-ko-BA-ga): Called the Hillsborough River today, located close to Tampa. Nearby, the Withlacoochee River leads northwest toward the Tallahassee area.
Tribute: A required payment that shows respect.
Tsala (TSA-la): A lake on the Withlacoochee River.
Tumpline: A strap that goes across the forehead to help support a pack carried on the back.
Waving crab: Fiddler crab that burrows into sand or mud. Male fiddler crabs have one extra-large claw to wave at female crabs. These tiny air-breathing crabs move to higher land to escape the rising waters that hurricanes bring.

Weir (weer): A fencelike trap placed across part of a river to catch fish. (See figure Q on page 52.)

Welfare: A government system for providing food and help for people in need.

Wetland: A low, wet area, such as a marsh or the edge of a river.

Whippoorwill: An insect-eating bird that repeats "whip-poor-will" in a continuing song on summer evenings.

Winters: The passing of one year's worth of time. For example, someone ten winters old would be ten years old.

Yamassee: A native group that lived in Georgia.

Zemis: A native word for "ceremonial mask," probably in the Arawak language. Arawak people lived on the island of Hispañola, located southeast of Florida.

References

Other Books about Florida Indians

Andrews, Evangeline, and Charles Andrews, eds. *Jonathon Dickinson's Journal or God's Protecting Providence.* Port Salerno, Fla.: Florida Classics Library, 1985.

Ashley, Keith, and Bob Richter. *Excavation of the Dent Mound (8Du68), Duval County, Florida.* Jacksonville: Jacksonville Museum of Science and History, 1993.

Blanchard, Charles. *New Worlds, Old Songs.* Gainesville: Institute of Archaeology and Paleoenvironmental Studies, University of Florida, 1995.

Blanchard, Charles, Nina Borremans, and Claudine Payne. *Florida Heritage Program Lesson Plans: Native People of Florida.* Tallahassee: Division of Historical Resources, Florida Department of State, 1996.

Borremans, Nina, and Michael Russo. "Florida's Historical Contexts." http://dhr.dos.state.fl.us/bar/hist_contexts/, accessed June 16, 2001.

Brown, Robin C. *Florida's First People.* Sarasota, Fla.: Pineapple Press, 1994.

Bullen, Ripley P. *A Guide to the Identification of Florida Projectile Points.* Gainesville: Kendall Books, 1975.

Burrage, D. D. *Early English and French Voyages, 1534–1608.* New York: Scribner's, 1906.

Caduto, Michael J., and Joseph Bruchac. *Keepers of the Animals.* Golden, Colo.: Fulcrum, 1991.

Cotterill, R. S. *The Southern Indians: The Story of the Civilized Tribes before Removal.* Norman: University of Oklahoma Press, 1989.

Culberson, Linda Crawford. *Arrowheads and Spear Points in the Prehistoric Southeast.* Jackson: University Press of Mississippi, 1993.

Dobyns, Henry F. *Their Number Become Thinned: Native American Population Dynamics in Eastern North America.* Knoxville: University of Tennessee Press, 1983.

The Domain of the Calusa: Archaeology and Adventure in the Discovery of South Florida's Past. Video. Main Sail Video Productions, 1995.

Duke, James A., and Stephen Foster. *Peterson Field Guides: Eastern/Central Medicinal Plants.* Boston: Houghton Mifflin, 1990.

Faupel, W. John, and Sarah Lawson. *A Foothold in Florida.* West Sussex, England: Antique Atlas, 1992.

Flint Knapping with Bruce Bradley, Ph.D. Video. INTERpark and Primitive Technology Graphics, 1989.

Florida Geographic Information Board. "Population by Race and Hispanic or Latino Origin, for All Ages and for 18 Years and Over, for Florida: 2000." http://www.floridacensus.com, accessed June 4, 2002.

Gannon, Michael. *The Cross in the Sand: The Early Catholic Church in Florida.* Gainesville: University Press of Florida, 1993.

Granberry, Julian. *A Grammar and Dictionary of the Timucua Language.* 3d. ed. Tuscaloosa: University of Alabama Press, 1993.

Hann, John H. *A History of the Timucua Indians and Missions.* Gainesville: University Press of Florida, 1996.

———. *Apalachee: The Land between the Rivers.* Gainesville: University Press of Florida, 1988.

———, ed. and trans. *Missions to the Calusa.* Gainesville: University Press of Florida, 1991.

Hann, John H., and Bonnie G. McEwan. *The Apalachee Indians and Mission San Luis.* Gainesville: University Press of Florida, 1998.

Hudson, Charles M. *The Southeastern Indians.* Knoxville: University of Tennessee Press, 1976.

———, ed. *Black Drink, a Native American Tea.* Athens: University of Georgia Press, 1979.

Hudson, Charles M., and Carmen Chaves Tesser, eds. *The Forgotten Centu-*

ries: Indians and Europeans in the American South, 1521–1704. Athens: University of Georgia Press, 1994.

Jones, Maxine D., and Kevin M. McCarthy. *African Americans in Florida*. Sarasota, Fla.: Pineapple Press, 1993.

Kelley, Todd. Interview by the author. Jacksonville, Fla., 1995.

Kozuch, Laura. *Sharks and Shark Products in Prehistoric South Florida*. Gainesville: Institute of Archaeology and Paleoenvironmental Studies, University of Florida, 1993.

Mails, Thomas E. *The Cherokee People*. New York: Marlowe, 1992.

Marquardt, William H., ed. *Culture and Environment in the Domain of the Calusa*. Gainesville: Institute of Archaeology and Paleoenvironmental Studies, University of Florida, 1992.

McCarthy, Kevin M. *Native Americans in Florida*. Sarasota, Fla.: Pineapple Press, 1999.

McEwan, Bonnie G., ed. *The Spanish Missions of La Florida*. Gainesville: University Press of Florida, 1993.

McGoun, William E. *Ancient Miamians*. Gainesville: University Press of Florida.

Milanich, Jerald T. *Archaeology of Precolumbian Florida*. Gainesville: University Press of Florida, 1994.

———. *Florida Indians and the Invasion from Europe*. Gainesville: University Press of Florida, 1995.

———. *Florida's Indians from Ancient Times to the Present*. Gainesville: University Press of Florida, 1998.

———. *The Timucua*. Oxford: Blackwell, 1996.

Milanich, Jerald T., and Susan Milbrath, eds. *First Encounters: Spanish Explorations in the Caribbean and the United States, 1492–1570*. Gainesville: University of Florida Press, 1990.

Milanich, Jerald T., and Samuel Proctor, eds. *Tacachale: Essays on the Indians of Florida and Southeastern Georgia during the Historic Period*. Gainesville: University Presses of Florida, 1978.

Milanich, Jerald T., and William C. Sturtevant. *Francisco Pareja's 1613* Confessionario*: A Documentary Source for Timucuan Ethnography*. Tallahassee: Division of Archives, History, and Records Management, Florida Department of State, 1972.

Morris, Craig. Interview by the author. Timucuan Ecological and Historic Preserve, National Park Service, Jacksonville, 1995.

National Oceanic and Atmospheric Administration, Office of Public Affairs, National Weather Service. "Weather Technology Services." http://www.nws.noaa.gov, accessed July 12, 2001.

Peterson, Lee Allen. *Peterson Field Guides: Edible Wild Plants.* Boston: Houghton Mifflin, 1977.

Powell, Terry. Interview by the author. Dunedin, Fla., April 2000.

Purdy, Barbara A., and Roy C. Craven, Jr. *Indian Art of Ancient Florida.* Gainesville: University Press of Florida, 1996.

Rogers, Michael. "Flint versus Chert: What's the Difference?" http://theacca.com, accessed February 6, 2002.

Schell, Rolfe. *1000 Years on Mound Key.* Ft. Myers, Fla.: Island Press, 1968.

Seminole Student Museum Staff. Interview by the author. Sanford, Fla., 1995.

Snow, Dean R. *The Iroquois.* Oxford: Blackwell, 1994.

Ste Claire, Dana. *True Natives: The Prehistory of Volusia County.* Daytona: Hall, 1992.

Walton, Richard K., and Robert W. Lawson. *Peterson Field Guides: Eastern/Central Birding by Ear.* Boston: Houghton Mifflin, 1989.

Weitzel, Kelley G. "Environmental Adaptation: The Shift from Paleo to Archaic Survival Strategies." http://pelotes.jea.com, accessed June 18, 2001.

———. "The Timucua Indians: After the Europeans Came." http://pelotes.jea.com, accessed June 18, 2001.

———. *The Timucua Indians: A Native American Detective Story.* Gainesville: University of Florida Press, 2000.

Worth, John E. *The Struggle for the Georgia Coast.* Atlanta: American Museum of Natural History, 1995.

———. *Timucua Chiefdoms of Spanish Florida.* Vol. 1, *Assimilation.* Vol. 2, *Resistance and Destruction.* Gainesville: University Press of Florida, 1998.

Index

Pages with illustrations are in **boldface**.

Kelley G. Weitzel is Senior Preserve Naturalist at the Pelotes Island Nature Preserve in Jacksonville, Florida, where she has taught about Florida nature and history for ten years. She is the author of *The Timucua Indians: A Native American Detective Story* (University Press of Florida, 2000).